A Note From Rick Renner

I am on a personal quest to see a "revival of the Bible" so people can establish their lives on a firm foundation that will stand strong and endure the test as end-time storm winds begin to intensify.

In order to experience a revival of the Bible in your personal life, it is important to take time each day to read, receive, and apply its truths to your life. James tells us that if we will continue in the perfect law of liberty — refusing to be forgetful hearers, but determined to be doers — we will be blessed in our ways. As you watch or listen to the programs in this series and work through this corresponding study guide, I trust you will search the Scriptures and allow the Holy Spirit to help you hear something new from God's Word that applies specifically to your life. I encourage you to be a doer of the Word He reveals to you. Whatever the cost, I assure you — it will be worth it.

> Thy words were found, and I did eat them;
> and thy word was unto me the joy and rejoicing of mine heart:
> for I am called by thy name, O Lord God of hosts.
> — Jeremiah 15:16

Your brother and friend in Jesus Christ,

Rick Renner

Ten Steps To Block the Devil From Your Life

How To Use This Study Guide

This ten-lesson study guide corresponds to *"Ten Steps To Block the Devil From Your Life" With Rick Renner* (**Renner TV**). Each lesson in this study guide covers a topic that is addressed during the program series, with questions and references supplied to draw you deeper into your own private study of the Scriptures on this subject.

To derive the most benefit from this study guide, consider the following:

First, watch or listen to the program prior to working through the corresponding lesson in this guide. (Programs can also be viewed at **renner.org** by clicking on the Media/Archives links.)

Second, take the time to look up the scriptures included in each lesson. Prayerfully consider their application to your own life.

Third, use a journal or notebook to make note of your answers to each lesson's Study Questions and Practical Application challenges.

Fourth, invest specific time in prayer and in the Word of God to consult with the Holy Spirit. Write down the scriptures or insights He reveals to you.

Finally, take action! Whatever the Lord tells you to do according to His Word, do it.

For added insights on this subject, it is recommended that you obtain Rick Renner's book *Fallen Angels, Giants, Monsters, and the World Before the Flood* and Rick's study Bible, *The Renner Interpretive Version: James and Jude — A Conceptual Interpretation of the Greek New Testament With Footnotes and Commentary.* You may also select from Rick's other available resources by placing your order at **renner.org** or by calling 1-800-742-5593.

TOPIC

Become a Child of God

SCRIPTURES

1. **John 10:10** — The thief cometh not, but for to steal, and to kill, and to destroy: I am come that they might have life, and that they might have it more abundantly.

2. **John 10:10 (*RIV*)** — The thief wants to get his hands into every good thing in your life. In fact, this pickpocket is looking for any opportunity to wiggle his way so deeply into your personal affairs that he can walk off with everything you hold precious and dear. And that's not all. When he's finished stealing all your goods and possessions, he'll take his plan to rob you blind to the next level by creating conditions and situations so horrible that you'll see no way to solve the problems except to sacrifice everything that remains from previous attacks. The goal of this thief is to totally devastate your life. If nothing stops him, he'll leave you insolvent, flat broke, and cleaned out in every area of your life. You'll end up feeling as if you're finished and out of business. Make no mistake. The enemy's ultimate aim is to obliterate you.

3. **Colossians 1:13** — Who hath delivered us from the power of darkness, and hath translated us into the kingdom of his dear Son.

4. **1 John 3:14** — We know that we have passed from death unto life....

5. **1 John 5:18** — We know that whosoever is born of God sinneth not; but he that is begotten of God keepeth himself, and that wicked one toucheth him not.

GREEK WORDS

1. "thief" — κλέπτης (*kleptes*): bandit, thief, or scam artist

2. "steal" — κλέπτω (*klepto*): one so artful in the way he steals that his exploits of thievery are nearly undetectable; a pickpocket; it is where we get the word kleptomaniac

3. "kill" — θύω (*thuo*): not kill, as in murder, but to sacrifice; to surrender or to give up something that is precious and dear

4. "destroy" — **ἀπόλλυμι** (*apollumi*): to devastate, destroy, ruin, trash, or waste

5. "life" — **ζωή** (*zoe*): associated with divine life; depicts life that is filled with gusto, zest, and vitality

6. "abundantly" — **περισσός** (*perissos*): abundantly; excessively; exceedingly; extraordinary; something that abounds in an extraordinary measure; so profuse that it can be likened to a river overflowing and flooding beyond its banks; overflowing, plentiful, or even superabundant

7. "delivered" — **ῥύομαι** *(rhuomai)*: to rescue, to deliver, to snatch, or even to drag out of danger; to save in the nick of time; a rescue operation intended to snatch a person out of physical or spiritual peril; intervention

8. "from" — **ἐκ** (*ek*): out, and it is where we get the word exit

9. "power" — **ἐξουσία** (*exousia*): authority; influence

10. "darkness" — **σκότος** (*skotos*): bleak darkness, or the darkest moment of the night; darkness, blackness, gloom, and a never-ending state of obscurity

11. "translated" — **μεθίστημι** (*methistemi*): from **μετά** (*meta*), denoting a change, turn, or transfer, and **ἵστημι** (*histemi*), which means to appoint, establish, or stand; as a compound, it means to remove or transfer and to stand firmly and securely

12. "kingdom" — **βασιλεία** (*basileia*): kingdom; realm of authority, domination, influence, and rule

13. "passed" — **μεταβαίνω** (*metabaino*): from **μετά** (*meta*), indicating a change, transition, or a turn, and the word **βάσις** (*basis*), meaning to walk; as a compound, it means to walk out a change; it pictures a full transition from one place to another place

14. "death" — **θάνατος** (*thanatos*): death, either physical or spiritual; can denote a death sentence

15. "life" — **ζωή** (*zoe*): life, either physical or spiritual; used in the New Testament to picture the life of God or divine life; a life full of gusto and zeal

16. "wicked one" — **ὁ πονηρὸς** (*ho poneros*): the malevolent, malignant, spiteful, wicked one

17. "touched" — **ἅπτομαι** (*haptomai*): to lay hold of, usually in a bad way

18. "not" — **οὐχ** (*ouch*): emphatically not

SYNOPSIS

The devil has been allowed to wreak havoc in our world today. Sin and lawlessness abound, yet many believe he is a non-existent, fictional character. But the devil is not a fantasy — he is real. This ten-lesson study, *Ten Steps To Block the Devil From Your Life*, will focus on the following important steps:

- Become a Child of God
- Receive the Baptism in the Holy Spirit
- Pray and Read Your Bible
- Have Strengthening Relationships
- Protect Your Marriage
- Invest Spiritually in Your Children
- Give Tithes and Offerings and Be Careful How You Spend Money
- Give No Place to Bitterness and Unforgiveness
- Eat Right and Exercise
- Be Filled With the Spirit

The emphasis of this lesson:

The first and most important step in blocking the devil's access to your life is to become a child of God. But you do have an enemy — the devil. And from the time he was cast out of Heaven, the devil's modus operandi has been to steal, kill, and destroy anything that belongs to God. The good news is, the day you make Jesus the Lord of your life, you are transferred from the kingdom of darkness and given a firm and secure standing in the kingdom of God from which to block the devil's access to your life!

Many people do not believe the devil exists, but his evil influence can be seen in many areas of the world and culture in which we live. Peter wrote that the devil is prowling, roaming, and searching for a way to attack and devour anyone who is vulnerable and ignorant of his schemes (*see* 1 Peter 5:8). The fact is, the devil is not a fantasy, and he will do everything he can to gain access to our lives.

The Kleptomaniac

In John 10:10 Jesus said,

> **The thief cometh not, but for to steal, and to kill, and to destroy: I am come that they might have life and that they might have it more abundantly.**

The word "thief" is translated from the Greek word *kleptes,* which describes *a bandit, a thief, or a scam artist,* and is where we get the English word "kleptomaniac." A kleptomaniac is one who just cannot keep himself from stealing because it is his very nature to steal. By using the word *kleptes,* Jesus in essence was saying, "Don't be surprised. The devil just can't help himself. He is flawed; he is defective. From the very beginning of time, he has been a thief. Something within him is bound and determined to take what belongs to someone else."

When we study history, we discover that the devil has *always* been a thief. He wanted the throne of God; he wanted God's position and tried to steal it. He wanted the adoration of the angels and tried to steal that adoration. Satan wanted Adam's position in the garden and tried to rob him of it. The devil is a thief, and he steals because it is his very nature to steal. But that's not all. John 10:10 says, "The thief cometh not, but for to *steal,* and to *kill,* and to *destroy....*"

Nearly Undetectable Thievery

The word "steal" in Greek is *klepto,* which is the active form of the word *kleptes.* The word *klepto* depicts *one so artful in the way he steals that his exploits of thievery are nearly undetectable.* It describes *a pickpocket.* The meaning behind John 10:10 can be expressed this way: "The kleptomaniac, when he shows up, will begin to behave like a kleptomaniac. He will be nearly undetectable. He can't restrain himself, and He'll steal and steal simply because it is his nature to steal."

If you have good health, the thief wants to steal your health. If you have a great job, he wants to take your job away from you. If you are walking in joy, he attempts to steal your joy. The devil doesn't steal because he needs any of it; he steals simply because he is a kleptomaniac who cannot keep himself from stealing what belongs to someone else. He is bound and determined to take whatever you have.

A Religious Sacrifice

Jesus continues to say in John 10:10 that not only does the thief come to steal, but he also comes to "kill." The word "kill" is translated from the Greek word *thuo*. It does not actually mean to kill, as in murder. The word *thuo* is a religious term meaning *to sacrifice, to surrender,* or *to give up something that is precious and dear.* But in the context of John 10:10, what does this really mean?

By using the word *thuo,* Jesus is informing us that there are times when the devil disguises himself to sound very pious and religious. He may try to deceive us by whispering something like, "There is no hope of restoration for you. There is no way you will be able to recover what has been lost. Why even try to believe? Just lay everything on the altar and give it all up. Simply sacrifice it and walk away."

In an attempt to convince you, the devil may even disguise his voice to sound like the voice of God and say things like, "There is no hope in believing or trying. Just give up, walk away, and surrender it all." If the thief hasn't already taken everything from you, he will attempt to coax you into giving up the fight of faith and walking away.

The Devil Wants To Unravel Our Lives

Not only does the devil want to steal from you and convince you to give up and walk away from God's promises, but he also wants to *destroy* you. The word "destroy" is a form of the Greek word *apollumi,* which means *to devastate, to destroy, to ruin, to trash,* or *to waste.*

The *Renner Interpretive Version (RIV)* of John 10:10 says,

The thief wants to get his hands into every good thing in your life. In fact, this pickpocket is looking for any opportunity to wiggle his way so deeply into your personal affairs that he can walk off with everything you hold precious and dear. And that's not all. When he's finished stealing all your goods and possessions, he'll take his plan to rob you blind to the next level by creating conditions and situations so horrible you'll see no way to solve the problems except to sacrifice everything that remains from previous attacks. The goal of this thief is to totally devastate your life. If nothing stops him, he'll leave you insolvent, flat broke, and cleaned out in every area of your life. You'll

end up feeling as if you're finished and out of business. Make no mistake. The enemy's ultimate aim is to obliterate you….

John 10:10 provides us with a vivid description of the nature and behavior of the devil. He is out to destroy *everyone* — both saved and unsaved.

Life More Abundantly

Jesus went on to say in John 10:10, "…I am come that they might have life, and that they might have it more abundantly." The word "life" used in this verse is a form of the Greek word *zoe* and depicts *a life that is filled with gusto, zest, and vitality.*

The Greek word for "abundantly" is *perissos*, which means *abundantly; exceedingly; an extraordinary life; something that abounds in an extraordinary measure; something so profuse that it can be likened to a river overflowing and flooding its banks; something that is overflowing, plentiful, or even superabundant.*

Jesus came to give us the very opposite of what the devil is determined to steal from us. As soon as we become a child of God, a block is built to stop the thief and destroyer from gaining access to our lives. Not only that, but Colossians 1:13 tells us that God "hath delivered us from the power of darkness, and hath translated us into the kingdom of his dear Son."

Our Exit From the Kingdom of Darkness

The word "hath" used in Colossians 1:13 is past tense, meaning the moment we called Jesus our Lord, we *were* transferred out of the kingdom of darkness and translated into the kingdom of God's Son. In that very moment, a divine transaction occurred. We were "delivered."

The word "delivered" is translated from the Greek word *rhuomai*, which means *to rescue, to deliver, to snatch,* or *to drag out of danger just in the nick of time.* It depicts *a rescue operation intended to snatch a person out of physical or spiritual peril.* The day we made Jesus the Lord of our life, a divine rescue operation occurred. God rescued us and snatched us from the power of darkness!

Colossians 1:13 says that God has "…delivered us from the power of darkness…." The word "from" in this verse is the Greek word *ek*, meaning "out," and it is where we get the English word "exit." Salvation was our *exit* from the power of darkness.

The word "power" in this verse is the Greek word *exousia*, which describes *authority* or *influence*. Once we make Jesus our Lord, darkness no longer has any authority in our life, and we have the power through Jesus to renounce any influence the devil may try to exert over us.

The Greek word for "darkness" is *skotos*, which describes *bleak darkness* or *the darkest moment of the night*. It depicts *blackness, gloom,* and *a never-ending state of obscurity*. This is where we were living before we called Jesus our Lord. But the *very moment* we surrendered to Jesus, our exit from that bleak darkness occurred as God rescued us! God literally snatched us from that place of dense darkness and gloom, and translated us into the kingdom of His dear Son!

Colossians 1:13 also says that God "hath translated us into the kingdom of his dear Son." The word "translated" is the Greek word *methistemi*. It is a compound of two words, *meta*, which denotes *change, a turn,* or *a transfer;* and *istemi*, which means *to appoint, to establish,* or *to stand*. As a compound Greek word, *methistemi* means *to remove or transfer and to stand firmly and securely*. In other words, once we have been transferred out of the kingdom of darkness, we have been given a firm and secure standing in the kingdom of God.

The word "kingdom" is a form of the Greek word *basileia*, which describes *a kingdom, a realm of authority, domination, influence,* and *rule*. The day we were saved, Jesus snatched us from the grip of the enemy and placed us under *His* rule and authority! When we declared Jesus as Lord, we made our exit from the kingdom of darkness and obscurity, and we were given a firm, secure standing in the kingdom of Jesus where He rules and reigns. For that reason, the devil should not be allowed access to our life.

Untouchable

First John 3:14 says, "We know that we have passed from death unto life…." The Greek meaning for the word "passed" is *to walk out a change* and pictures *a full transition from one place to another place*. We have made a full transition out of the domain of darkness and death and have walked directly into life. This is our new status!

Additionally, First John 5:18 says, "We know that whosoever is born of God sinneth not; but he that is begotten of God keepeth himself, and that wicked one toucheth him not." When we have been put in Christ, and we live according to the Word of God, we position ourselves out of the reach of the enemy. However, if we make wrong choices that are contrary to God's Word, the door will be opened to provide the devil access to our life.

The Greek word for "wicked" is *ho poneros*, describing *the malevolent, malignant, spiteful, wicked one*. The word "toucheth" in First John 5:18 is from the Greek word *haptomai*, meaning *to lay hold of, usually in a bad way*.

The word translated "not" in First John 5:18 is the Greek word *ouch*, which is the most emphatic form of the English word "not." This means the devil will *not* be able to lay a hand on us if we obey the Word of God, keep ourselves in His will, and are rooted in Christ.

When we become a child of God, a spiritual barricade is erected around us, stopping the thief — the one who steals, kills, and destroys — from finding access to our life! When we become a child of God, we are snatched from the kingdom of darkness — we make our exit from that evil kingdom — and are placed firmly and securely into the kingdom of God. We pass from death into life, and if we stay in God's Word and choose to obey the Bible, the devil will be unable to lay his hand on us!

QUESTIONS AND ANSWERS WITH RICK RENNER

In the program, Rick answered the following question from one of our viewers.

Q. Are there female angels or baby cherub angels?

A. The answer to both is *no*. From the beginning to the end of the Bible, we never find one example of a female angel or a cherub. The ancient artwork depicting sweet little baby cherubs with wings was used as an incentive in the old world to encourage people to procreate. And if you study most cults that exist today — and cults that existed in ancient times — you will find that most of them were started by a "female angel" who brought some kind of new teaching or revelation.

When a person claims to have seen a female angel, he or she needs to take heed and be cautious because it is a sure sign that person is listening to a spirit that was not sent from God. Again, there are no female angels, and there are no little sweet baby cherubs with wings found in the Bible.

STUDY QUESTIONS

**Study to shew thyself approved unto God, a workman that needeth
not to be ashamed, rightly dividing the word of truth.
— 2 Timothy 2:15**

1. Describe the meaning of "thief" in John 10:10 and explain why this word is important for every child of God to understand.

2. Explain how the Greek words for "thief" and "steal" are related.

3. Based on the meaning of "kill" in John 10:10, what is one way the devil disguises himself?

PRACTICAL APPLICATION

**But be ye doers of the word, and not hearers only,
deceiving your own selves.
— James 1:22**

1. Read John 10:10 and describe the life Jesus died to provide for His followers. Note the areas of your life where you are experiencing the *zoe* life Jesus spoke about.

2. Examine your own life and note the areas in which you are *not* experiencing the fullness of what Jesus provided. Then read James 4:7 and First John 5:18. What is one change you will make in your life today to block the devil from your life.

LESSON 2

TOPIC

Receive the Baptism in the Holy Spirit

SCRIPTURES

1. **Matthew 3:11** — I indeed baptize you with water unto repentance: but he that cometh after me is mightier than I, whose shoes I am not worthy to bear: he shall baptize you with the Holy Ghost, and with fire.

2. **Luke 3:16** — John answered, saying unto them all, I indeed baptize you with water; but one mightier than I cometh, the latchet of whose shoes I am not worthy to unloose: he shall baptize you with the Holy Ghost and with fire.

3. **John 20:21,22** — … Peace be unto you: as my Father hath sent me, even so send I you. And when he had said this, he breathed on them, and saith unto them, Receive ye the Holy Ghost.

4. **Luke 24:49** — And, behold, I send the promise of my Father upon you: but tarry ye in the city of Jerusalem, until ye be endued with power from on high.

5. **Acts1:4-5** — And, being assembled together with them, commanded them that they should not depart from Jerusalem, but wait for the promise of the Father, which, saith he, ye have heard of me. For John truly baptized with water; but ye shall be baptized with the Holy Ghost not many days hence.

6. **Acts 1:8** — But ye shall receive power, after that the Holy Ghost is come upon you: and ye shall be witnesses unto me both in Jerusalem, and in all Judaea, and in Samaria, and unto the uttermost part of the earth.

7. **Luke 10:19** — Behold, I give unto you power to tread on serpents and scorpions, and over all the power of the enemy: and nothing shall by any means hurt you.

GREEK WORDS

1. "baptize" — βαπτίζω (*baptidzo*): a word that originally meant to dip and dye; in early usage, it described the process of dipping a cloth or garment into a vat of color to dye it, leaving it there long enough for the material to soak up the new color and then pulling that garment out of the dye with a permanently changed outward appearance; to baptize; to fully immerse

2. "endued" — ἐνδύω (*enduo*): the act of putting on a garment or a piece of clothing; presents the idea of sinking into a garment and becoming at ease in it; the usage of this word means certain traits will be operative only when they are deliberately picked up, put on by choice, as one would dress himself in a new set of clothes

3. "power" — δύναμις (*dunamis*): power; explosive, superhuman power that comes with enormous energy and produces phenomenal, extraordinary, and unparalleled results; depicts "mighty deeds" that

are impressive, incomparable, and beyond human ability to perform; miraculous power or miraculous manifestations; used to denote the full might of an advancing military army; used to describe the effect of earthquakes, hurricanes, and tornadoes or a force of nature

4. "shall receive" — **λαμβάνω** (*lambano*): to seize or to lay hold of something in order to make it your very own, almost like a person who reaches out to grab, to capture, or to take possession of something; at other times, it depicts one who graciously receives something that is freely and easily given

5. "behold" — **ἰδού** (*idou*): amazement, bewilderment, shock, and wonder

6. "over" — **ἐπί** (*epi*): over or upon, denoting a superior position

7. "all" — **πᾶσαν** (*pasan*): all; an all-inclusive term meaning all and everything, excluding nothing

8. "enemy" — **ἐχθρός** (*exthros*): pictures one who holds an adversarial position of extreme hostility

9. "nothing" — **οὐδὲν** (*ouden*): absolutely nothing

10. "by any means" — **οὐ μὴ** (*ou me*): no or not; stresses that nothing — no, nothing — shall hurt you

11. "hurt" — **ἀδικέω** (*adikeo*): to abuse, to harm, to injure, or to maltreat

SYNOPSIS

In Lesson 1, we discovered that becoming a child of God was the foundational and most important step in blocking the devil's access to our life. The second step is the baptism in the Holy Spirit. When we receive this powerful gift, we become so infused with the third member of the Godhead that even in the face of every obstacle through which the devil endeavors to find an entrance into our life, we have the power to overcome.

The emphasis of this lesson:

Our great enemy, the devil, is looking for any crack in the foundation of our lives to enter through. But we have been given explosive, superhuman power through the baptism in the Holy Spirit to close every door, bar every window, and seal every crack and block him from all access!

In John 14:30, Jesus said, "…The prince of this world cometh, and hath nothing in me." Jesus knew the devil would come to tempt Him. But He also knew that because He lived uprightly, every crack, door, and window into His life were slammed closed. There was absolutely *no* access point in Jesus' life for the devil to enter through. In the same way, when we live right and do right by the power of God's Word and the Holy Spirit, the devil is denied access to our lives! As we move forward in this study, we will continue to explore ten ways we can block the devil's access into our lives.

Be Baptized in the Holy Spirit

On the program, Rick explained that when he was growing up, he did not even know that there was such a gift as the baptism in the Holy Spirit. He knew about the Holy Spirit's gift of salvation, but his knowledge was limited concerning the third member of the Godhead. Rick had been taught about Heaven, but he was ignorant about the power of God; he had no knowledge about the authority he had over the devil. In fact, Rick didn't even really believe there was a devil — he thought the devil was just a mythical character. So as Rick struggled through life, he had the *peace* of God, but he did not have any *power* to help him overcome life's obstacles.

Jesus and others in the New Testament spoke very clearly about a second experience called the baptism in the Holy Spirit. In Matthew 3:11, John the Baptist declared, "I indeed baptize you with water unto repentance...." He was referring to salvation. Then John continued, "...But he that cometh after me is mightier than I, whose shoes I am not worthy to bear: he shall baptize you with the Holy Ghost, and with fire." John was telling those listening that beyond water baptism, there is a second baptism.

In Luke 3:16, Luke recounts the same instance in a slightly different way: "John answered, saying unto them all, I indeed baptize you with water; but one mightier than I cometh, the latchet of whose shoes I am not worthy to unloose: he shall baptize you with the Holy Ghost and with fire."

Fully Immersed

As recorded in Matthew 3:11 and Luke 3:16, John the Baptist spoke of a mightier one coming after him — Jesus Christ. John also declared that Jesus would baptize us in the Holy Ghost and fire.

The Greek word for "baptize" is *baptidzo*, and the original meaning is *to dip and dye*. In early usage, it described the process of dipping a cloth or garment into a vat of color to completely dye it, leaving the cloth or garment in the dye long enough for the material to soak up the new color, and then pulling the garment out of the dye with a permanently changed outward appearance. It means *to baptize* or *to fully immerse.*

People are often confused by the difference between being baptized *by* the Spirit into Christ and being baptized *in* the Holy Spirit. First Corinthians 12:13 says, "For by one Spirit are we all baptized into one body...." We are all baptized *by* the Holy Spirit into Christ the moment we are saved. When we call Jesus the Lord of our life, the Holy Spirit miraculously takes us and melds us or baptizes us into the person of Christ. In a flash, by the work of the Holy Spirit, we become a member of the Body of Christ.

Three Baptisms

There are three baptisms found in the Bible:

1. The baptism of salvation, which is when the Holy Spirit baptizes us into the Body of Christ.
2. The baptism in the Holy Spirit, which is when Jesus baptizes us into the power of God.
3. The baptism in water, which when another believer baptizes us into water to signify that we have received Jesus Christ as Lord and Savior.

Immersed Into the Holy Spirit

When Jesus baptizes us, He immerses us so deeply into His Spirit that we become completely saturated with the Spirit of God. We become so infused that we are suddenly enabled to live a Spirit-filled life. Even in the face of every obstacle, we have the power to overcome anything the devil would try to throw our way. This is a necessary step in blocking the devil from having access to our lives.

Baptized Into the Body of Christ

John 20:21 and 22 records that when Jesus' disciples were saved, Jesus said to them:

> **Peace be unto you: as my Father hath sent me, even so send I you. And when he had said this, he breathed on them, and saith unto them, Receive ye the Holy Ghost.**

The phrase "he breathed on them," is the Greek word *emphusao* and literally means *breathed into them at that very moment*. The tense of this Greek word means Jesus was saying, "Right now — at this very moment — receive the Holy Ghost." This is the moment the Spirit of God entered the hearts of the disciples, and they were saved and baptized into the body of Christ.

Endued With Power

It is important to note that the account recorded in John 20:21 and 22 is not describing the baptism of Jesus in the power of the Holy Spirit — it is describing *salvation*. But days later, as recorded in Luke 24:49, Jesus instructed His disciples to wait in the city of Jerusalem until they were "endued with power from on high."

Luke 24:49 says,

> **And, behold, I send the promise of my Father upon you: but tarry ye in the city of Jerusalem, until ye be endued with power from on high.**

The Greek word for "behold" is *idou*, which means *"Wow, listen to this!"* Jesus was very excited about what He was about to share with them. The word "endued" is a form of the Greek word *enduo*, which describes the act of putting on a garment or piece of clothing and presents the idea of sinking into that garment and becoming at ease in it. The usage of this word clearly means certain traits will be operative only when they are deliberately picked up and put on by choice, as one would dress himself in a new set of clothes. Jesus' desire is not merely to baptize us in the Holy Spirit; He wants us to dress in the power of the Holy Spirit until we sink into that experience and become comfortable with the power of God.

Dunamis

The word "power" found in Luke 24:49 is a form of the Greek word *dunamis*. It describes *power* or *explosive superhuman power that comes with enormous energy and produces phenomenal extraordinary and unparalleled results*. The word *dunamis* also depicts mighty deeds that are impressive, incomparable and beyond human ability to perform. It is the very word used in the New Testament to describe *miracles* or *miraculous manifestations*. This word was also used in the First Century to depict *the full might of an advancing military army* or to describe *the effects of an earthquake, hurricane, tornado or force of nature*. This is the type of power we receive when Jesus baptizes us in the Holy Spirit — which is a *secondary* experience that follows salvation.

Acts 1:4 and 5:

> **And, being assembled together with them, commanded them that they should not depart from Jerusalem, but wait for the promise of the Father, which, saith he, ye have heard of me. For John truly baptized with water; but ye shall be baptized with the Holy Ghost not many days hence.**

The word "commanded" indicates that this is not an option. Jesus then describes the "promise," which is that they will be baptized in the Holy Ghost.

You Shall Receive Power

Jesus continues in Acts 1:8,

> **But ye shall receive power, after that the Holy Ghost is come upon you: and ye shall be witnesses unto me both in Jerusalem, and in all Judea, and in Samaria, and unto the uttermost part of the earth.**

Those Jesus was addressing were already saved. Jesus had already breathed the Spirit into them, but He was explaining how the Spirit would come upon them and dress them in supernatural power. Jesus would soon baptize them, immersing them in the power of the Holy Spirit until they were saturated, soaked, and settled into it — as if it were a set of new clothes.

When Jesus stated, "Ye shall receive power," the phrase He used for "receive power" is a form of the Greek word *lambano*, which means *to seize* or *to lay a hold of something in order to make it your very own*. It also depicts *one who graciously receives something that is freely and easily given*. Jesus has given us the baptism in the Holy Spirit, but we must receive it by faith. When we do receive the baptism in the Holy Spirit, we receive power.

Another important verse is Luke 10:19, which says,

> **Behold, I give unto you power to tread on serpents and scorpions, and over all the power of the enemy: and nothing shall by any means hurt you.**

The word "over" is the Greek preposition *epi*, which means *over or upon*. This word denotes *a superior position*. The power of God gives us the upper hand over the devil.

The word "all" is the Greek word *pasan* which is an all-inclusive term meaning *all and everything, excluding nothing*. The word "power" in this verse is again the Greek word *dunamis*. That means there will be times when the devil comes against us with all he has — and it may feel like a hurricane — but Jesus said that we have been given authority over *all* the power of the enemy.

The word "enemy" is the Greek word *exthros*, which pictures *one who holds an adversarial position of extreme hostility*. The devil hates all humans because we are made in the image of God. The reason he wants to strike us is because when he attacks us, he is attacking the very image of God.

'Nothing Shall by Any Means Hurt You'

When Jesus said, "…Nothing shall by any means hurt you," the Greek word He used for "nothing" is *ouden*, which literally means *absolutely nothing at all, by any means*. In addition to the Greek word *ouden*, there are two small Greek words: *ou*, which means *no*; and *me*, which means *not*. When all three words are used together, the literal meaning is *no, not nothing*. This is a very abrasive statement. Jesus was really saying, "Nothing. No, not nothing shall hurt you."

The word "hurt" is a form of the Greek word *adikeo*, which means *to abuse, to harm, to injure*, or *to maltreat* and is exactly what the devil desires to do to us. He wants to abuse us, harm us, injure us, and maltreat us. And he is looking for any open door, window, or crack to gain access to our lives to do it. But if we are born again and have received the power of the Holy Ghost, we have the upper hand and we have been placed in a superior position so that *nothing shall by any means hurt us*.

It is absolutely essential that we receive the baptism in the Holy Spirit. The Holy Spirit will help block the devil from our lives. And if the devil has already gained access, we have the power and authority of the Holy Spirit to completely push him out of our lives!

QUESTIONS AND ANSWERS WITH RICK RENNER

In the program, Rick answered the following question from one of our viewers.

What language did Jesus speak, and what languages did He know?

A. Growing up in Israel, Jesus would have been familiar with Latin, and He would have known Hebrew because it was used in a religious context. Jesus would have also known Aramaic, but because of the influence of Alexander the Great, the people of Israel had primarily spoken Greek for 300 years before the time of Jesus.

In fact, they spoke so much Greek that by Jesus' time, most people were not able to read the New Testament in the Hebrew language. That is the reason the scholars in Alexandria took the Hebrew scriptures and translated them into the Greek version called the Septuagint. Scholars wanted the people to read the Old Testament, but because they could no longer read Hebrew, it was translated into the Greek language, which was the commonly spoken language of the *entire world* during the time Jesus was alive.

STUDY QUESTIONS

> Study to shew thyself approved unto God, a workman that needeth not to be ashamed, rightly dividing the word of truth.
> — 2 Timothy 2:15

1. According to Matthew 3:11 and Luke 3:16, who baptizes born again believers in the Holy Spirit?
2. List the three types of baptism found in the Bible and briefly describe each one.
3. When Jesus appeared to His disciples in Luke 24:49, He instructed them to remain in the city of Jerusalem until they had been "endued with power from on high." Describe the Greek meaning of the word "endued."

PRACTICAL APPLICATION

**But be ye doers of the word, and not hearers only,
deceiving your own selves.
— James 1:22**

1. In Luke 24:49 Jesus said, "And, behold, I send the promise of my Father upon you: but tarry ye in the city of Jerusalem, until ye be endued with power from on high." If you have asked Jesus into your heart and are a child of God but have never heard of or received the baptism in the Holy Spirit — which is the power from on high to which Jesus is referring — pray and ask to receive this powerful gift today. Read and meditate on Jesus' words in this Luke 24:49.

2. If you have been baptized in the Holy Spirit, list two ways you have seen His power at work in your personal life as a result.

TOPIC

Pray and Read Your Bible

SCRIPTURES

1. **Psalm 5:3** — My voice shalt thou hear in the morning, O Lord; In the morning will I direct my prayer unto thee, and will look up.

2. **1 Thessalonians 5:17** — Pray without ceasing.

3. **Ephesians 6:18 (*AMPC*)** — Pray at all times (on every occasion, in every season)....

4. **2 Timothy 3:16,17 (*TLB*)** — The whole Bible was given to us by inspiration from God and is useful to teach us what is true and to make us realize what is wrong in our lives; it straightens us out and helps us do what is right. It is God's way of making us well prepared at every point, fully equipped to do good to everyone.

5. **Proverbs 30:5** — Every word of God is pure: he is a shield unto them that put their trust in him.

6. **Psalm 119:11** — Thy word have I hid in mine heart, that I might not sin against thee.

7. **Psalm 119:24** — Thy testimonies also are my delight and my counselors.
8. **Psalm 119:80** — Let my heart be sound in thy statutes; that I be not ashamed.
9. **Psalm 119:98** — Thou through thy commandments hast made me wiser than mine enemies: for they are ever with me.
10. **Psalm 119:105** — Thy word is a lamp unto my feet, and a light unto my path.
11. **Psalm 119:130** — The entrance of thy words giveth light; it giveth understanding unto the simple.
12. **Psalm 119:154** — Plead my cause, and deliver me: quicken me according to thy word.

GREEK WORDS

1. "without ceasing" — ἀδιαλείπτως (*adialeiptos*): without interruption, without taking a break, or continuously

SYNOPSIS

The devil is searching for an entrance into our life. It might be through our health, finances, wrong thinking, marriage, children, or any number of areas. But God has given us the ability to close every access point. One avenue to block his entrance into our lives is as simple as praying and reading the Bible daily. In this lesson, we will explore these specific weapons to block the devil's access.

The emphasis of this lesson:

The two most important habits to establish in our daily lives that block the devil's interference are prayer and reading the Bible. In Psalm 5:3 David said, "My voice shalt thou hear, O Lord; in the morning will I direct my prayer unto thee, and will look up." It is important to pray God's Word and pray *without ceasing*. David began his day by praying, and we should do the same.

The apostle Paul said in Ephesians 4:27, "...neither give place to the devil." The word "place" is the Greek word *topos* and describes *an actual geographical location*. This is not a mythical place. The devil is looking for an *actual* place — an access or entry point into our life. That access may be through our marriage, health, finances, wrong thinking, or even looking at something inappropriate. The devil is searching for any crack where he can wiggle his way into our lives, but we can stop him. This is a very, very practical teaching that can easily be applied to our daily walk with the Lord.

In previous lessons, we learned that the first step is to become a child of God and the second step is to receive the baptism in the Holy Spirit. The third step is very simple: pray and read the Bible every day. Most of the attacks in our lives are a result of a lack of prayer and not reading the Bible daily. The Bible teaches that the Word of God is a shield to those who live in it.

Look Up To Start Your Day

King David wrote in Psalm 5:3,

> **My voice shalt thou hear in the morning, O Lord; in the morning will I direct my prayer unto thee, and will look up.**

David had been the king of Israel for 40 years. He had been a powerful king but had not been without trouble in his life. David had troubles in his marital relationship, with his sons, with his relatives, with his associates, and with various people in his kingdom. The book of Psalms records David's highs and lows, but an important lesson he learned was that if he was going to have a good day, he needed to begin his day by *looking up*.

Establish a Daily Habit of Prayer

On the program, Rick told the following story:

> During a very difficult time in my life, I neglected praying and reading my Bible daily. I was doing the work of the ministry, and Denise and I were traveling back and forth between two cities because we were pastoring two churches in those two cities. We were going non-stop and would actually have times when we would wake up in the middle of the night and say, 'Where are we? What city are we in?' I would have moments where I couldn't find the bathroom because I was confused about where we were. We were just going through the motions, almost like robots, living on airplanes and traveling through different time zones — back and forth, back and forth. It was unwise for us to live at this pace,

and I became physically, mentally, and spiritually drained. In that depleted state, I began to make mistakes.

I knew I was in trouble, so I called for the elders of our ministry — men who had authority and oversight of our ministry — and asked for help. They came to Moscow and met with us and helped us design a new plan for our life. They examined how we had been living. They said, 'Rick, the reason you've been open to attack is because what you're doing is impractical and unreasonable. No one can live like this.' The first change I made was to establish a daily habit of prayer, and I made the decision that I would begin every day with prayer.

That does not mean that I spend hours and hours in prayer every day. It simply means that before I ever lift my head from my pillow or put my feet on the ground, I begin to go through a list of daily prayers.

First, I welcome the presence of God and thank Him for His work in my life. The Bible says in the morning we are to thank Him for His lovingkindness. I also thank God for His faithfulness and pray for my own spiritual growth. I pray for Denise who is lying next to me. I pray for our sons and their wives. I pray for all of our grandchildren by name. Then I begin to pray for my spiritual team. I pray for all of my staff. I pray for our friends and partners. I pray specifically for some of our very dear friends. I go through this list every single day before I ever lift my head from the pillow.

It may sound like this will take a long, long time, but it doesn't. It takes just a few moments. By looking up, I've guaranteed that I have started my day in the right direction. I have learned in my personal life that if I don't look up as I begin my day, things inevitably spiral downward.

Rather than start my day negatively, I have determined that I'm going to practice what David practiced in his life as recorded in Psalm 5:3, which says, 'My voice shalt thou hear in the morning. O Lord; In the morning will I direct my prayer unto thee, and will look up.'

Some may be thinking, *Well, I am just not a morning person. I can't practice this in my life.* But that is not true. If you decide to begin your day by spending time with the Lord, He will enable you to maximize the rest of your day.

Many believers waste so much time. Ask yourself how much time you spend watching TV, surfing the Internet, or looking on social media. All of these activities waste precious time in your life. Why don't you go to bed a little earlier so you can wake up earlier and spend time with the Lord before starting your day? Establishing this habit will help you block the devil from finding access into your life. Through your fellowship with the Lord, you will develop ears to hear Him warn you about areas where the devil is trying to attack. By listening to the Lord in prayer, you can block the devil's access into your life.

Pray at All Times

Prayer should become a lifestyle for us. The purpose of prayer is not just to check off a spiritual box. We are told in First Thessalonians 5:17 to "pray without ceasing." This does not mean we must go about our day with our eyes closed, praying from morning until evening. Instead, it describes a *mental* mindset of staying in a state of prayer.

The words "without ceasing" in Greek mean *without interruption, without taking a break,* or *continuously.* It is an attitude of staying in fellowship and communication with the Lord at all times that is similar to the way Rick begins his day with prayer before he ever gets out of bed or lifts his head from his pillow.

When you read the Bible, ask the Holy Spirit to open the Word to you. When you walk into work, ask the Lord to guide your steps. Constantly communicate with the Lord. When you sit at your desk, pray that God would help you be effective, efficient, and productive. Choose to actively be in communication with Him. Living this way will give you ears to hear so the Lord can warn you about any area the devil is trying to access in your life, allowing you to block his efforts.

Ephesians 6:18 (*AMPC*) says,

Pray at all times (on every occasion, in every season)....

You can pray for your spouse and your marriage. You can pray for your children and your grandchildren. You can pray for your leaders, including your pastor and local leaders. You can pray for the president of the nation. You can pray for your unsaved friends and family members. You can pray for financial provision and God's favor. You can pray for revelation and understanding of the Word of God. You can pray for angelic protection over your home. It is so easy to pray, and there are so many things to pray about. Don't wait until you're in a crisis before you pray.

A Double-Edged Sword

Prayer is so vital, but another very important area in blocking the devil from gaining access into our lives is God's Word. In addition to praying each morning, we must make time for reading the Word of God. His Word is a shield to us.

There is no other resource in the world like the Word of God — it is a double-edged sword (*see* Hebrews 4:12). You can read many other books, but when you read the Bible, the Bible reads you. The Word will reveal areas in your life that you need to adjust and change. If you allow the Word to speak to you — *and you obey it* — it will block the enemy from gaining access to your life. If you have a Bible in every room in your house, as many Christians do, don't just look at those Bibles and let them collect dust. Pick one up, open it, and begin to read a little bit every day.

The Benefits of God's Word

Second Timothy 3:16 and 17 (*TLB*) says,

> **The whole Bible was given to us by inspiration from God and is useful to teach us what is true and to make us realize what is wrong in our lives; it straightens us out and helps us do what is right. It is God's way of making us well prepared at every point, fully equipped to do good to everyone.**

God's Word will teach us truth and reveal areas in our life that we need to change while giving us strength to do what is right. Through God's Word, we will be well prepared and enabled to do good for others.

Proverbs 30:5 states,

> **Every word of God is pure: he is a shield unto them that put their trust in Him.**

The implication of this verse is that by reading the Word of God, living it, and trusting in it, we will be shielded from every attack of the devil.

Psalm 119:11 says,

Thy word have I hid in mine heart, that I might not sin against thee.

This means that when the Word is active in our lives, we will be less likely to sin.

Psalm 119:24 says,

Thy testimonies also are my delight and my counselors.

The Word of God will counsel us in every situation, helping us block the devil's access to our life.

In Psalm 119:80, the psalmist states,

Let my heart be sound in thy statutes; that I be not ashamed.

The Word of God will make us mentally sound, which is so important considering the world in which we live today.

Psalm 119:98 says,

Thou through thy commandments hast made me wiser than mine enemies.

The Word of God will make us wise, wiser than those motivated by the devil.

Psalm 119:105 is familiar to many:

Thy word is a lamp unto my feet, and a light unto my path.

When we need guidance, the Word of God provides it.

Psalm 119:130 says,

The entrance of thy words giveth light; it giveth understanding unto the simple.

God's Word will bring illumination whenever we need it. It will give us understanding, and if we are physically, spiritually, and mentally depleted, it will quicken us. Psalm 119:54 states, "Plead my cause, and deliver me: quicken me according to thy word." God's Word has quickening power. It will revive us in every area of our life.

Sometimes people who are in ministry make the mistake of thinking that preparing a message or listening to a message preached by another person will be sufficient for their daily spiritual sustenance. But that is not the case. Every child of God, whether in ministry or not, needs to hear directly from God. It is vital for all of us to have a daily intake of God's Word into our life.

If it feels like reading the Bible is difficult or that you have hit a dry season and the particular version of the Bible you are currently reading is not speaking to you, there are plenty of other translations. Find a version that speaks to you. Each day, be determined to set aside time to read God's Word, and let Him speak to you as you read.

QUESTIONS AND ANSWERS WITH RICK RENNER

In the program, Rick answered the following question from one of our viewers.

Q. Is the husband the only one who should be in charge of the budget for a family's finances?

A. When I was growing up, my father was in charge of the family budget, but honestly, we really struggled financially. My dad believed that as head of the home, he should pay all the bills and be in charge of the family finances. But later in life, my mother said to him, "Ronald, let me take a hand at that."

When my mother began to manage the family finances, everything changed. Dad was so sorry that he had not allowed Mother to do that earlier. My opinion is that the one who handles the family finances may depend on who has the best gift to do it. The husband is the head of the home, and it is important for the husband and wife to be in agreement about who does the finances.

STUDY QUESTIONS

Study to shew thyself approved unto God, a workman that needeth not to be ashamed, rightly dividing the word of truth.
— 2 Timothy 2:15

1. According to Psalm 5:3, what are two benefits of directing our prayers to the Lord "in the morning"?
2. Explain the meaning of First Thessalonians 5:17 and describe how it is possible to "pray without ceasing."
3. Read Psalm 119:11-25; 80-105; 130; 159. List three ways in which daily reading of God's Word benefits our lives.

PRACTICAL APPLICATION

**But be ye doers of the word, and not hearers only,
deceiving your own selves.
—James 1:22**

1. Take a moment to examine your prayer life. What steps can you take to improve or increase your conversations with the Lord?
2. Read Psalm 119:105 and describe its meaning in your own words. In what ways have you seen this truth about the Word of God operating in your life?

LESSON 4

TOPIC

Have Strengthening Relationships

SCRIPTURES

1. **Psalm 54:4** — Behold, God is mine helper: the Lord is with them that uphold my soul.
2. **Proverbs 11:14** — Where no counsel is, the people fall: but in the multitude of counsellors there is safety.
3. **Proverbs 24:6** — For by wise counsel thou shalt make thy war: and in multitude of counsellors there is safety.
4. **Proverbs 13:20** — He that walketh with wise men shall be wise: but a companion of fools shall be destroyed.
5. **Proverbs 17:17** — A friend loveth at all times, and a brother is born for adversity.

6. **Proverbs 18:24** — A man that hath friends must shew himself friendly: and there is a friend that sticketh closer than a brother.

7. **Proverbs 27:17** — Iron sharpeneth iron; so a man sharpeneth the countenance of his friend.

8. **Ecclesiastes 4:9-12** — Two are better than one; because they have a good reward for their labour. For if they fall, the one will lift up his fellow: but woe to him that is alone when he falleth; for he hath not another to help him up. Again, if two lie together, then they have heat: but how can one be warm alone? And if one prevail against him, two shall withstand him; and a threefold cord is not quickly broken.

9. **John 15:12,13** — This is my commandment, That ye love one another, as I have loved you. Greater love hath no man than this, that a man lay down his life for his friends.

10. **Hebrews 10:25** — Not forsaking the assembling of ourselves together, as the manner of some is; but exhorting one another: and so much the more, as ye see the day approaching.

11. **Galatians 6:2** — Bear ye one another's burdens, and so fulfill the law of Christ.

GREEK WORDS

1. "forsake" — ἐγκαταλείπω (*egkataleipo*): compound of ἐν (*en*), κατα (*kata*), and λείπω (*leipo*); the word ἐν (*en*) means in; the word κατα (*kata*) means down and out; the word λείπω (*leipo*) means behind, as in to be behind everyone else; it pictures one who is discouraged, defeated, and depressed; it depicts the emotions of a person who feels left out, down, depressed, and far behind everyone else

2. "exhorting" — παρακαλέω (*parakaleo*): to urge, beseech, plead, beg, or pray; it pictures one who comes closely alongside another person to speak to him, console him, comfort him, or assist him with counsel or advice; used to depict military leaders who came alongside their troops to exhort and plead with them to stand tall and face their battles bravely

3. "bear" — βαστάζω (*bastadzo*): to carry, to lift up, or to bear something; to bear a responsibility

4. "burdens" — βάρος (*baros*): a weight that is heavy or crushing; could refer to a physical problem, circumstantial problem, or spiritual prob-

lem; a burden far too heavy to carry alone; if one attempts to carry it alone, it could be crushing

SYNOPSIS

The first and most important step to block the devil from your life is to become a child of God. Step two is to receive the baptism in the Holy Spirit. Step three is to pray and read our Bible every day. The next very important step to block the devil from our life is to have strong relationships. No one can stand alone; we need relationships. Part of building strong friendships is being committed to a Bible-believing church. We need to encourage one another, especially as the day is approaching — the day of the rapture of the Church (*see* Hebrews 10:25).

The emphasis of this lesson:

Developing strengthening relationships is imperative to blocking the devil from accessing our lives. Just like the Roman soldiers needed each other to stand shoulder to shoulder and resist the approaching enemy armies, we need godly relationships and influences as we stand against every attack of the devil. Strengthening relationships enable us to build a spiritual barricade, denying the devil access into our life.

Standing Together

In Psalm 54:4, King David wrote,

> **Behold, God is mine helper: the Lord is with them that uphold my soul.**

Most people are so independently minded that they only focus on the first part of this psalm, "God is mine helper...." But David continued by describing *how* the Lord helped him, "the Lord is with them that uphold my soul." One way God helps us and upholds our soul is by bringing people into our life who will stand with us. When others are standing with us, even when hell is coming against us, we are able to resist the inroads of the enemy.

The Roman army was very wise and developed a special battle strategy called the tortoise technique. This strategy involved soldiers linking their shields, first on the front and then over the top covering their heads, soldier to soldier. Through this technique, the Roman army would create a front so strong that enemy armies could not penetrate them. This formation was significantly stronger than one soldier standing alone.

The reason God puts people into our life is so we are not doing life alone. We all need people to encourage us and to celebrate our victories with us.

Safety in a Multitude of Counselors

We are more prone to making mistakes when we are left to ourselves. Proverbs 11:14 warns,

> **Where no counsel is, the people fall: but in the multitude of counsellors there is safety.**

Counsel comes from the people in our life. It is important to have friendships that are not just periphery people. We need relationships that are central figures in our life. In the multitude of counselors and solid, covenant friends, there is safety.

Similarly, Proverbs 24:6 says,

> **For by wise counsel thou shalt make thy war: and in multitude of counsellors there is safety.**

We cannot make war against the enemy alone because our vision is limited. When we have counselors, they help us make war correctly. We need people in our lives to create a buffer and aid us in advancing wisely.

Proverbs 13:20 says,

> **He that walketh with wise men shall be wise....**

When we have wise people speaking into our life, we will make wise decisions.

The Importance of Godly Friends

Proverbs 17:17 states,

> **A friend loveth at all times, and a brother is born for adversity.**

On the program, Rick explained how he has precious family members and brothers in Christ who are true spiritual brothers to him. He has friends who have loved him at all times and were born for a time of adversity.

These friends have been with him through thick and thin, so he has not had to face things alone.

Proverbs 18:24 says,

> **A man that hath friends must shew himself friendly: and there is a friend that sticketh closer than a brother.**

There are times when our friends in Christ are closer to us than our natural family members.

Proverbs 27:17 says,

> **Iron sharpeneth iron; so a man sharpeneth the countenance of his friend.**

When we have good covenant-friends in our life, they sharpen us and they make us better.

Ecclesiastes 4:9-12 says,

> **Two are better than one; because they have a good reward for their labour. For if they fall, the one will lift up his fellow: but woe to him that is alone when he falleth; for he hath not another to help him up. Again, if two lie together, then they have heat: but how can one be warm alone? And if one prevail against him, two shall withstand him; and a threefold cord is not quickly broken.**

The wisdom of Solomon is expressed in this passage from Ecclesiastes, which tells us that we are not supposed to do life alone — two are better than one.

John 15:12 and 13 says,

> **This is my commandment, That ye love one another, as I have loved you. Greater love hath no man than this, that a man lay down his life for his friends.**

When we see someone lay down their life for us, not only does it impact us, it makes us want to lay down our own life for someone else. We are supposed to be laying down our life for others, but we should also have those in our life who are willing to lay down their life for us. We need people who we are accountable to — people who will love us through the best and worst moments in life. Who do you have in your life watching out for your soul? It is important to identify those individuals. You also need to identify those God has entrusted to you whose souls you are watching over.

A Divine Support Structure

Hebrews 10:25 says,

> **Not forsaking the assembling of ourselves together, as the manner of some is; but exhorting one another: and so much the more, as ye see the day approaching.**

According to this verse, some people have developed a habit of not attending church and avoiding fellowship.

The word "forsaking" in Hebrews 10:25 is a Greek word that is composed of three words. It is a triple compound comprised of the Greek words *en*, *kata*, and *leipo*. The word *en* means *in*, and the word *kata* means *down and out*. The word *leipo* means *behind, as to be behind everyone else*. When these words are compounded to make the word *egkataleipo*, it pictures *one who is discouraged, feeling defeated and depressed*. The word depicts *the emotions of a person who feels left out, down, depressed, and far behind everyone else*. Being in that state, this person starts avoiding fellowship.

Often when people need encouragement the most, they hide and isolate themselves from others. They avoid church because people will be talking about victory, and they don't feel victorious themselves. They know people will be raising their hands in worship to God and they don't want to do that. The very thing they need, they avoid. Because they are depressed, they no longer attend church. But this is the most important time to be in church! We need the strength of others. We need a united front to help block the advance of the enemy in our life.

We also need to be actively connected to a good, solid, Spirit-filled church that teaches the Bible. We need to sit in the presence of the anointing. Those things strengthen us and reinforce us spiritually as we stand against the enemy. We all need the support structure of a local church and of trusted friends who care about us and who will speak the truth in love to us — *especially* when we are discouraged, defeated, and feeling depressed.

The Day Approaching

Again, Hebrews 10:25 says, "Not forsaking the assembling of ourselves together, as the manner of some is; but exhorting one another: and so much the more, as ye see the day approaching." The phrase "the day approaching" refers to the coming of the Lord and implies that the closer we come to the rapture of the church, the more we will need encouragement. There will be opportunities to become discouraged because of the onslaught of evil. We are seeing this happening all around the world today. We need a united front of people in our life to stand with us, especially during the times in which we are living, to completely block the access of the enemy.

The word "exhorting" in this passage is a form of the Greek word *parakaleo*. It means *to urge, to beseech, to plead, to beg,* or *to pray*. It pictures *one who comes closely alongside another person*. It describes *someone who comes closely to speak, comfort, and assist another with counsel or advice*. This Greek word is the very word used to depict military leaders who came alongside their troops to exhort and plead with them to stand tall and face the battle bravely.

Who do you have like that in your life? Everyone needs a person like this. When you're tempted to bow out and give in to your flesh or your emotions, you need someone to say, "Hold on, hold your head up, throw your shoulders back, and stand. You can do what you have been called to do. You're going to make it through this." We need someone to celebrate us in good times and encourage us in bad times. That is the reason this verse tells us to exhort one another.

Reciprocal Encouragement

Our close relationships should be reciprocal, not just one-sided. Stop for just a moment and identify those people in your life who speak into your life, encourage you, celebrate with you, and speak difficult words of truth when you need to hear those words. Who gives you counsel and advice and encourages you to stand tall and face your battles bravely? Identify those people who watch out for your soul. Now flip that question around and ask yourself, *How am I being that person for someone else?*

We all need people who will speak into our lives and friendships in which we can share honestly and candidly with each other. You may say, "Well, I have no idea how to be in contact with anyone regularly so we can share in this way."

This is easier than it may seem. You don't need to communicate with your friends for hours at a time — an email, a text message, or just a quick call is all it takes. If you have ever read Rick and Denise's autobiography, *Unlikely*, you know that they have faced many battles through the years and it was very *unlikely* that they should have survived. But one big reason Rick and Denise have been able to stay the course for so long is there have been people who have stood with them and connected their spiritual "shields" in a united front. When we are standing with other believers, even if the enemy tries to penetrate our defenses, he will not be successful, because of those who stand with us.

QUESTIONS AND ANSWERS WITH RICK RENNER

In the program, Rick answered the following question from one of our viewers.

Q. What is your favorite place in Scripture?

A. I read something from the book of Psalms every single day of my life. In the book of Psalms, there is comfort, there is strength, and there is healing for the soul. I would encourage you to make the reading of the book of Psalms a part of your daily Bible reading. Even if you only read one psalm, always include a Psalm because it will bring strength and comfort into your life. The book of Psalms will also release healing into your life. I would have to say the book of Psalms is a very critical part of my daily Bible reading.

STUDY QUESTIONS

Study to shew thyself approved unto God, a workman that needeth not to be ashamed, rightly dividing the word of truth.
— 2 Timothy 2:15

1. Describe how the Romans were able to successfully resist their enemies in battle and explain how that compares to our walk with the Lord.

2. Read Proverbs 18:24, Proverbs, 27:17, and Ecclesiastes 4:9-12. What does God's Word have to say about friendship?

3. Explain Psalm 54:4 in your own words and how you will apply it to your life.

PRACTICAL APPLICATION

But be ye doers of the word, and not hearers only,
deceiving your own selves.
—James 1:22

1. Think about the people in your life who "uphold your soul." Take a moment to pray for them and ask the Lord for an encouraging word to share with them.

2. What is one psalm from the Bible that God has used to minister to you and explain how it has personally impacted your life.

LESSON 5

TOPIC

Protect Your Marriage

SCRIPTURES

1. **Genesis 2:15** — And the Lord God took the man, and put him into the garden of Eden to dress it and to keep it.

2. **Proverbs 24:30-34** — I went by the field of the slothful, and by the vineyard of the man void of understanding; and, lo, it was all grown over with thorns, and nettles had covered the face thereof, and the stone wall thereof was broken down. Then I saw, and considered it well: I looked upon it, and received instruction. Yet a little sleep, a little slumber, a little folding of the hands to sleep: so shall thy poverty come as one that traveleth; and thy want as an armed man.

3. **Proverbs 24:30-34 (AMP)** — I went by the field of the lazy man, and by the vineyard of the man lacking understanding and common sense; and, behold, it was all overgrown with thorns, and nettles were covering its surface, and its stone wall was broken down. When I saw, I considered it well; I looked and received instruction. "Yet a little sleep, a little slumber, a little folding of the hands to rest [and daydream]," Then your poverty will come as a robber, and your want like an armed man.

4. **Ecclesiastes 4:9-12** — Two are better than one; because they have a good reward for their labour. For if they fall, the one will lift up his fellow: but woe to him that is alone when he falleth; for he hath not another to help him up. Again, if two lie together, then they have heat: but how can one be warm alone? And if one prevail against him, two shall withstand him; and a threefold cord is not quickly broken.

5. **Proverbs 30:5** — Every word of God is pure: he is a shield unto them that put their trust in him.

6. **Proverbs 13:20 (*NLT*)** — Walk with the wise and become wise; associate with fools and get in trouble.

GREEK WORDS

1. "dress" — Hebrew, to cultivate, develop, nurture, serve, or work
2. "keep" — Hebrew, to guard, hedge about, circumspectly keep, preserve, protect, or to make sure; also carries the idea of watchfulness

SYNOPSIS

One major area in which the devil will try to infiltrate our personal affairs is through our marriage. In the Garden of Eden, God instructed Adam to "dress" and "keep" it. God gave Adam the responsibility to develop, nurture, serve, and work the garden he had been given. He was also instructed to preserve, protect, and watch over what he had been given. Adam failed because he did not communicate properly with Eve. He did not protect what God had given him — the gift of Eve. Marriage is a gift from God, and we must be determined to cultivate and guard it.

The emphasis of this lesson:

Adam failed to watch over and cultivate the precious garden he had been given. Your marriage is also a precious gift from God that must be watched over. In this lesson, we will cover six major ways to cultivate your marriage.

The devil is searching for any crack or open door in our spiritual foundation to gain access to our lives. His intention is to steal, kill, and destroy anything he can in order to bring chaos into our lives. The devil hates that we have been made in God's very image and likeness, and by attacking us, the devil believes he is attacking God Himself.

In previous lessons, we have studied steps we can take to block the devil's access to our lives. Step one is to become a child of God. Step two is to receive the baptism in the Holy Spirit. The third step is to pray and read the Bible daily. Step four is to have strengthening relationships. And in this lesson, we will study step five, which is to protect our marriage.

To Dress and To Keep

Genesis 2:15 says,

> **And the Lord God took the man, and put him into the garden of Eden to dress it and to keep it.**

When God placed man in the garden, His first purpose for man was for him to "dress" the garden. The Hebrew word for "dress" means *to cultivate, develop, nurture, serve,* and *work* something. Most people would imagine that the Garden of Eden was perfect. However, God expects us to cultivate, develop, and increase anything He has given us. God gave Adam the responsibility of cultivating the garden that had been given to him; he was to develop, nurture, serve, and work it.

Genesis 2:15 also records that man was to "keep" the garden. The word "keep" means *to guard, to build a hedge about, to circumspectly keep, to preserve, to protect,* or *to make sure.* This word carries the idea of *watchfulness.* God expected man to be very serious about keeping the garden, which means God knew there was a sinister enemy lurking who would try to find his way into the garden.

Genesis 2:15 could be translated, "And the Lord God took the man and put him into the Garden of Eden to cultivate, develop, nurture, serve, work, guard, build a hedge about, circumspectly keep, preserve, protect, make sure, and be watchful over it."

God knew the enemy would try to get into the garden, so He essentially said to Adam, "Not only are you to cultivate the garden, develop it, nurture it, serve it, and work it, but I also want you to *guard* it. I want you to protect it and preserve it — really be watchful because there's an enemy who will try to find his way into the garden."

Proverbs 24:30-34 says,

> **I went by the field of the slothful, and by the vineyard of the man void of understanding; and, lo, it was all grown over with**

thorns, and nettles had covered the face thereof, and the stone wall thereof was broken down. Then I saw, and considered it well: I looked upon it, and received instruction. Yet a little sleep, a little slumber, a little folding of the hands to sleep: So shall thy poverty come as one that traveleth; and thy want as an armed man.

This same passage in the *Amplified* version reads,

I went by the field of the lazy man, and by the vineyard of the man lacking understanding and common sense; and, behold, it was all overgrown with thorns, and nettles were covering its surface, and its stone wall was broken down. When I saw, I considered it well; I looked and received instruction. 'Yet a little sleep, a little slumber, a little folding of the hands to rest [and daydream],' then your poverty will come as a robber, and your want like an armed man.

The meaning of this passage from Proverbs is if we don't take care of what has been given to us by God, it will fall to pieces. And when it falls apart, we will feel like we have lost everything. We may even complain, saying the devil has attacked us. But the truth is, we opened the door to his attacks by our lack of diligence over what has been given to us from God.

Proverbs 24:30-34 perfectly describes what happened with Adam and Eve as recorded in Genesis 2:15. Adam neglected to cultivate, develop, nurture, work at, and serve the garden. Adam was to guard it, keep it, protect it, and to be watchful over it because He knew the enemy would try to find a way in.

In the very same way, we need to understand that marriage is a gift from God. God knew it was not good for us to do life alone. Solomon wrote about the importance of not doing life solo in Ecclesiastes 4:10-12, which says, "For if they fall, the one will lift up his fellow: but woe to him that is alone when he falleth; for he hath not another to help him up. Again, if two lie together, then they have heat: but how can one be warm alone? And if one prevail against him, two shall withstand him; and a threefold cord is not quickly broken."

Two Are Better Than One

God knew that Adam needed a partner. He knew that two are better than one. In fact, God said, 'It is not good that the man should be alone...' (Genesis 2:18).

If we have a spouse, it is a blessing. However, if we have not treated our marriage like it is a garden entrusted to us from God, we may find the condition of it in shambles. It is our responsibility to cultivate our marriage, to serve it, and to work at it. The devil will do everything he can to get between us and our spouse to bring destruction to our marriage.

In addition to our marriage, the devil can affect our children and our finances. And if allowed, his influence may even result in divorce. But these attacks can be avoided if we are determined to work at, cultivate, develop, serve, and circumspectly guard our marriage.

Six Ways To Cultivate Your Marriage

On the program, Rick shared six practical actions we can take to develop and cultivate our marriage:

Pray together.

Praying with your spouse doesn't need to take hours and hours. When I awake in the morning, if Denise is awake, I reach over and take her hand. I may say something like, 'Denise, let's acknowledge the presence of God.' Denise and I begin our day by praying together. Sometimes prayer only lasts one or two minutes, but it forms a very strong spiritual connection between the two of us. It is so important for us to pray together with our spouse.

Read and share the Bible with each other.

Both spouses need to be individually reading the Bible for themselves. By doing so, it causes each person to be spiritually sensitive to the Holy Spirit, which will enhance their marriage.

At some point, share with your spouse what you have gleaned from your daily Bible reading. Denise and I do that nearly every day. We don't take an hour to share; we simply share our thoughts. I may say, 'Denise, I was reading Psalm 119 this morning, and wow, this really impacted me.' Denise, in turn, will say, 'Well,

I was reading the book of Galatians.' She will then share with me what impacted her. It is healthy for us to share our thoughts about what we are receiving from the Word of God. By sharing the Word of God with each other, it causes the Word of God to remain central in our marriage.

Proverbs 30:5 says, 'Every word of God is pure; he is a shield unto them that put their trust in Him.' The inference of this verse is that God's Word is a shield. When we put the Word of God in our marriage, it guards and shields our marriage.

Talk every day.

It is amazing the number of married people who don't talk with each other. A lack of communication is often the door through which the devil finds his way into our marriage. Talk every day.

You may ask, 'Talk about what?' Just talk! Talk about what you did today. Talk about your schedule for the day. Talk about your plans for the day. Denise and I do this every day. Talk about your kids if you need to. Talk about your job. Talk about your projects. Talk about your mutual family goal. Just determine to talk with each other. Simply talking creates an open channel and is vital in developing, cultivating, and nourishing our marital relationship.

Do something recreational together.

You may immediately say, 'Well, I don't know what we're going to do that is recreational.' Honestly, it is really a challenge for Denise and me because we live in Moscow. There is no mall nearby. To go to a mall really takes some effort. There is so much traffic in Moscow that it is a little challenging to do recreational activities. Even though it is challenging, Denise and I have found some recreational activities to do together at home. We sit around the table and play Yahtzee or Sequence! We have so much fun playing these games and it is such a break from our schedule. I love to watch Denise play Yahtzee. She gets so excited when she rolls the dice and gets a 'Yahtzee.' I have actually learned how to win the game of Sequence and Denise is always trying to figure it out. We have so much fun together. Playing games is recreational and very good for us. We need to keep in mind that not only are we spirits, but we also have souls and physical bodies. Every part of us needs attention.

Go somewhere together.

It is important that you go somewhere together. If you can get to a mall, go. If you can't get to a mall or take a vacation, take a drive together and just enjoy the scenery. Go visit a friend or just get a cup of coffee together — but do something to break the monotony of your schedule and bring a little interest into your relationship.

Choose people with strong marriages to be your friends.

The Bible tells us in Proverbs 13:20 (*NLT)*, 'Walk with the wise and become wise; associate with fools and get in trouble.' If you do not have a strong marriage, spend time with people who do and observe and emulate how they treat one another.

There are no perfect marriages — *none*. But God's desire is for us to have the very best marriages we can have. We need to view our marriage like a garden that has been entrusted to us by God. Rather than allowing it to be overrun and fall into shambles, we can say, "Lord, You have given me this marriage, and I am going to keep the devil out by cultivating, developing, and working at my marriage. I am going to guard my marriage and build a hedge about it. I am determined to do these things to keep the devil out of my marriage."

If we will just use common sense and implement some of these simple actions, we can build a strong marriage and block the way for the devil to enter in. But if your marriage is already in trouble, the power of God is able to restore it!

QUESTIONS AND ANSWERS WITH RICK RENNER

In the program, Rick answered the following question from one of our viewers.

Q. What is the difference between a righteous person and a holy person?

A. That is a very wise question. The Bible tells us in Second Corinthians 5:21 that if you are in Christ, you have become the righteousness of God. That is a gift given to you. God declared you righteous because of your faith in Jesus. There are many righteous Christians who are not living a very holy life.

Holiness has to do with your lifestyle. There are many righteous people who are doing unholy things. God is calling us to live up to the level of our righteousness, and God declared us to be righteous.

Righteousness is a gift; holiness is your conduct.

STUDY QUESTIONS

Study to shew thyself approved unto God, a workman that needeth not to be ashamed, rightly dividing the word of truth.
— 2 Timothy 2:15

1. List the two responsibilities God gave to Adam concerning the Garden of Eden and explain the meaning of each.
2. Explain how Adam failed in the responsibilities God had given him in the Garden.
3. List six practices you can implement to cultivate your marriage.

PRACTICAL APPLICATION

But be ye doers of the word, and not hearers only, deceiving your own selves.
— James 1:22

1. In your own words, explain Proverbs 24:30-34. Is there an area in your life where you have been lazy? What is your plan to correct it?
2. If you are married, examine your relationship with your spouse. Explain how you will implement at least one of these suggestions from this lesson into your marriage. If you are single, choose one of the suggestions given and implement it into a close relationship in your life.

TOPIC

Invest Spiritually in Your Children

SCRIPTURES

1. **Psalm 127:3-5** — Lo, children are an heritage of the Lord: and the fruit of the womb is his reward. As arrows are in the hand of the mighty man; so are children of the youth. Happy is the man that hath his quiver full of them; they shall not be ashamed, but they shall speak with the enemies in the gate.

2. **Proverbs 22:6** — Train up a child in the way he should go: and when he is old, he will not depart from it.

3. **Galatians 6:7,8 (*MSG*)** — ...What a person plants, he will harvest. The person who plants selfishness, ignoring the needs of others — ignoring God! — harvests a crop of weeds. All he'll have to show for his life is weeds! But the one who plants in response to God, letting God's Spirit do the growth work in him, harvests a crop of real life, eternal life.

4. **Mark 8:36** — For what shall it profit a man, if he shall gain the whole world, and lose his own soul?

GREEK WORDS

1. "train up" — Hebrew, depicts taste buds and palate; taste refers to the basic sensations of sweet, sour, salty, and bitter that we experience with the tongue, while palate refers to the overall sensory experience of food and drink, including taste, aroma, texture, and even temperature

2. "child" — Hebrew, a youngster in formative years

3. "way [he should go]" — Hebrew, path, road, or way

4. "old" — Hebrew, mature or an aged and older person

5. "depart" — Hebrew, to eschew, to go aside, or to leave, but when used in a spiritual sense, it depicts apostasy or one leaving the way of faith

SYNOPSIS

Of all of the investments we make throughout our lives, investing spiritually into the lives of the children God has entrusted to us is of utmost importance. We must expose our children to God's presence, His Word, and His Spirit so they will develop an appetite for the things of God. He has given His promise that when those children are old, even if they depart from those things for a time, they will come back to Him.

The emphasis of this lesson:

When we invest spiritually in the lives of our children, the fruit of their lives will become a blessing in ours. The spiritual seeds we plant in their lives will result in a harvest of spiritual fruit that will enrich the world around them.

The devil is searching for any way he can gain access into our personal affairs. If he can find a way in, he will do everything he can to bring chaos and destruction into our lives. In previous lessons, we covered the first five steps to block the devil from gaining access to our life, which are to become a child of God, to receive the baptism in the Holy Spirit, to pray and read the Bible daily, to have strengthening relationships, and to protect our marriage. In this lesson, we will be examining the sixth step, which is to invest spiritually in our children.

Invest in the Spiritual Lives of Your Children

Psalm 127:3-5 tells us,

> **Lo, children are an heritage of the Lord: and the fruit of the womb is his reward. As arrows are in the hand of a mighty man; so are children of the youth. Happy is the man that hath his quiver full of them: they shall not be ashamed, but they shall speak with the enemies in the gate.**

God intends for our children to be a blessing to our life. So much so that Psalm 127:3-5 promises when we take time to spiritually invest in our children, they will deal with our enemies when we are older. When we invest spiritually in our children, they bless our lives. According to this passage, children are a heritage of the Lord — a gift from God.

Even if you made the mistake of *not* investing in your children when they were young, you can simply ask God to forgive you. You may even need to ask your children to forgive you for not doing a better job as a parent. But it is not too late! You can still invest spiritually in their lives.

For our children to produce good fruit, we must invest in their lives. As parents, we cannot sit back and just hope our children will grow up to be great adults. It is imperative that we plant the right seeds in the hearts of our children if we expect to have a good harvest from them. Building a Christ-centered foundation for our children is essential.

Train Up a Child

Proverbs 22:6 promises,

> **Train up a child in the way he should go: and when he is old, he will not depart from it.**

The phrase "train up," is a Hebrew word that describes *taste buds* and the *palate.* The word "taste" refers to *the most basic sensations of sweet, sour, salty, and bitter experienced with the tongue.* The word "palate" refers to *the overall sensory perception of food and drink, including taste, aroma, texture, and even temperature.*

Simply put, the phrase "train up" means that we are to give our children the right spiritual "taste buds" for God. It is our responsibility as parents to give our children sensory perception of the way they should go.

The word "child" in Hebrew describes *a youngster in his formative years* and the phrase "the way he should go" describes *the path, the road,* or *the way* he should go.

Proverbs 22:6 continues, "...and when he is old, he will not depart from it." The word "old" describes *one who is mature, one who is aged,* or *one who is older,* and the word "depart" means *to go aside, to leave,* or when used in a spiritual sense, it depicts *apostasy* or *one leaving the way of faith.*

What an amazing promise from God! When our children are young, if we give them a taste for the things of God, a taste for Jesus, a taste for the Word of God, and a taste for loving and serving the church, we can hold on to this promise from God. He promises us that when our children are older, even if they depart for a time, they *will return* to what they tasted and experienced when they were young!

Cultivating a Taste for the Spiritual

Denise and Rick were raised very differently from each other as far as food was concerned. Denise grew up on a small farm in northeastern Oklahoma, and her family grew their own corn, cucumbers, tomatoes and other vegetables. They ate the vegetables they grew, and in her home, they never had soft drinks and rarely ate sweets. Today, Denise eats — *and enjoys* — the same kinds of things she ate as a child. Why? Because in her formative years, her tastebuds developed a taste for what her parents fed her.

Rick's mother, on the other hand, gave him a taste for the things of God but did *not* give him a taste for eating healthy food. His mother fed their family fried and greasy food, sugar-loaded cereals, fast food, and potato chips of all kinds. In fact, they ate so many potato chips that when they went grocery shopping, they didn't buy just one bag, they bought an entire carton with an assortment of chips!

Rick's family often ate bologna sandwiches and canned vegetables, and Rick loved to eat TV dinners. They regularly drank sugar-loaded drinks and ate sugar-filled desserts. They put margarine on nearly everything they ate. In fact, Rick never tasted real butter until he was about 20 years old! They were so addicted to sugar that when they ate cantaloupe, they would remove the seeds and load it with sugar! Guess what Rick's adult taste buds liked and craved? Sweets, chips, and greasy, junky, fried food!

When Rick and Denise were first married, they did not see eye to eye concerning what they would eat. Denise wanted to feed him healthy food from their garden, but his response would always be, "I am not eating that food." He wanted fried, greasy, unhealthy food because he did not have a taste for what Denise was eating or what she wanted him to eat. Today Denise still eats like she ate as a child and Rick is still tempted to eat the unhealthy food he and his family ate.

In the very same way, we must develop our children's spiritual taste buds for God's Word, the presence of God, and faithful church attendance. God promises that if we correctly develop our children's spiritual taste buds when they are young, they will return to spiritual things when they are old. We must give our children such a wonderful experience with God that even if they depart for a season, they come back to the things of God when they are older.

If you have young children or grandchildren, read the Bible to them. Use Bibles that are filled with colorful pictures. When Rick was a child, his mother read to him every night from her book of Bible stories. He loved the stories, but it was the pictures that made the characters and events come alive. His mother would also buy lively, animated audio recordings of Bible stories that he would listen to over and over. It caused the Word of God to come alive in him. On the program, Rick said that he still cherishes those memories to this day and knows that the love he has for the Bible was developed in his spiritual taste buds by his mother.

Galatians 6:7 and 8 (*MSG*) says,

> ...What a person plants, he will harvest. The person who plants selfishness, ignoring the needs of others — *ignoring God!* — harvests a crop of weeds. All he'll have to show for his life is weeds! But the one who plants in response to God, letting God's Spirit do the growth work in him, harvests a crop of real life, eternal life.

Planting the right seeds in the hearts of our children and grandchildren, especially in their formative years, is so vital. We must take every opportunity to give our children an experience with God that will leave them with a taste for the things of God — so they will *always* return to Him.

Church Attendance Is Not Optional

Do not make the tragic mistake of saying, "Well, I'll just wait to teach my kids when they are older." Many Christian parents today are making the mistake of saying, "Well, I don't want to force my kids to go to church just because I go to church." That is nonsense. Do we ask our kids in the morning if they want to go to school? No. We don't give them the option of staying home. If we give our children the choice of going to school or staying home to sleep, watch TV, and play video games, most children will choose to skip school. That is the way the flesh behaves. It always gravitates toward selfishness.

If that is true about school, it is true about church, which is a spiritual education. Some parents raise their children to be intelligent, educated, and successful in an earthly profession but do not teach them spiritual truth. As a result, many of these children grow up and walk away from God. They may be educated and making money, but they are headed for hell. Jesus told us there is no profit for us if we gain the whole world but lose our soul (*see* Mark 8:36).

Remember, Proverbs 22:6 is our promise from God that we can hold onto:

Train up a child in the way he should go: and when he is old, he will not depart from it.

The best way to block the devil's access into the lives of our children and grandchildren is to develop their spiritual tastebuds for the things of God. Our time with our children during their formative years is temporary; the time passes quickly. We must be determined to expose our children and grandchildren to the things of God and block the devil's entrance into their lives.

QUESTIONS AND ANSWERS WITH RICK RENNER

In the program, Rick answered the following question from one of our viewers.

Q. Why did Jesus sweat blood in the Garden of Gethsemane?

A. That is referred to in Luke 22:44, which says, "And being in an agony he prayed more earnestly: and his sweat was as it were great drops of blood falling down to the ground." The word "agony" is translated from the Greek word *agonidzo*, from the root word *agon*, which describes *a wrestling match*. Jesus was engaged in a wrestling match between His will and His Spirit. He had to come to the place where He was surrendered to the will of God.

Luke 22:44 says, "...And His sweat was as it were great drops of blood falling down to the ground." Medical science has examined this and determined that Jesus was experiencing an actual medical condition in which a person feels such excruciating *mental* pressure, that his or her body begins to respond as if it is under *physical* pressure. In fact, when this occurs, the perceived physical pressure is so real that the top layer of skin separates from the second layer, and that vacuum fills with blood, which then oozes through the pores of the skin as a mixture of sweat and blood.

The very fact that this term is used tells us that when Jesus was praying in the Garden of Gethsemane, He was in the midst of the wrestling match of His life, and He was under great mental pressure as He was surrendering to go to the Cross.

STUDY QUESTIONS

Study to shew thyself approved unto God, a workman that needeth not to be ashamed, rightly dividing the word of truth.
— 2 Timothy 2:15

1. Read Proverbs 22:6 and explain the meaning of the words "train up."
2. Why is it so important to plant spiritual seeds in the hearts of our children, especially when they are young?

PRACTICAL APPLICATION

But be ye doers of the word, and not hearers only, deceiving your own selves.
—James 1:22

1. If you are currently raising children, list three ways you are investing spiritually in their lives.
2. If you do not have children of your own, list three ways you will invest spiritually in the lives of the children in your life (grandchildren, nieces, nephews, friends' children, siblings, cousins, students, etc.) or your future children.
3. If you have adult children who are no longer living in your home, pray and ask the Holy Spirit to help you find ways you can invest in their lives. Remember, *it's not too late!*

LESSON 7

TOPIC

Give Tithes and Offerings, and Be Careful How You Spend Money

SCRIPTURES

1. **John 10:10** — The thief cometh not, but for to steal, and to kill, and to destroy: I am come that they might have life, and that they might have it more abundantly.

2. **John 10:10 (*RIV*)** — The thief wants to get his hands into every good thing in your life. In fact, this pickpocket is looking for any opportunity to wiggle his way so deeply into your personal affairs that he can walk off with everything you hold precious and dear. And that's not all. When he's finished stealing all your goods and possessions, he'll take his plan to rob you blind to the next level by creating conditions and situations so horrible that you'll see no way to solve the problems except to sacrifice everything that remains from previous attacks. The goal of this thief is to totally devastate your life. If nothing stops him, he'll leave you insolvent, flat broke, and cleaned out in every area of your life. You'll end up feeling as if you're finished and out of business. Make no mistake. The enemy's ultimate aim is to obliterate you.

3. **Malachi 3:7-11** — Even from the days of your fathers ye are gone away from mine ordinances, and have not kept them. Return unto me, and I will return unto you, saith the Lord of hosts. But ye said, Wherein shall we return? Will a man rob God? Yet ye have robbed me. But ye say, Wherein have we robbed thee? In tithes and offerings. Ye are cursed with a curse: for ye have robbed me, even this whole nation. Bring ye all the tithes into the storehouse, that there may be meat in mine house, and prove me now herewith, saith the Lord of hosts, if I will not open you the windows of heaven, and pour you out a blessing, that there shall not be room enough to receive it. And I will rebuke the devourer for your sakes, and he shall not destroy the fruits of your ground; neither shall your vine cast her fruit before the time in the field, saith the Lord of hosts.

4. **Philippians 4:19** — But my God shall supply all your need according to his riches in glory by Christ Jesus.

5. **Philippians 4:19 (*RIV*)** — But my God will supply all your needs so completely that He will eliminate all your deficiencies. He will meet all your physical, tangible needs until you're so full, you have no more capacity to hold anything else. He will supply all your needs until you're totally filled, packed full, and overflowing to the point of bursting at the seams and spilling over.

GREEK WORDS

No Greek Words were shown on the TV program.

SYNOPSIS

One of the steps in denying the devil access into our lives is in the area of finances. There are many believers who love God but have been struggling for years in the financial areas of their lives. Tithing, giving offerings, and having a budget are all principals that will be examined in detail in this lesson.

The emphasis of this lesson:

Malachi 3 gives us the key to the "windows of Heaven" being opened in our lives for the release of God's financial blessings. When put into practice, it opens the door for God to rebuke the devourer for our sake and close the door to the devil wreaking havoc in our finances.

The Thief

The devil is a thief, and he would love to get his hands on our money. Most of us, at one time or another, have probably found our finances in a mess because the door to our life was left open to allow the devil access. He will take any opportunity he can find because it is simply his nature to steal.

Jesus clearly stated in John 10:10,

> **The thief cometh not, but for to steal, and to kill, and to destroy: I am come that they might have life, and that they might have it more abundantly.**

The *Renner Interpretive Version (RIV)* of John 10:10 says it this way:

> **The thief wants to get his hands into every good thing in your life. In fact, this pickpocket is looking for any opportunity to wiggle his way so deeply into your personal affairs that he can walk off with everything you hold precious and dear. And that's not all. When he's finished stealing all your goods and possessions, he'll take his plan to rob you blind to the next level by creating conditions and situations so horrible that you'll see no way to solve the problems except to sacrifice everything that remains from previous attacks. The goal of this thief is to totally devastate your life. If nothing stops him, he'll leave you insolvent, flat broke, and cleaned out in every area of your life. You'll**

end up feeling as if you're finished and out of business. Make no mistake. The enemy's ultimate aim is to obliterate you.

Tithes and Offerings

One way the devil can gain access to our finances is by our failure to give tithes and offerings. This can open the door for poverty to come rushing into our finances.

Some may argue that the tithe isn't found in the New Testament. But the truth is, the tithe is both an Old and New Testament principle. The tithe was established *before* the law of Moses and is a spiritual principle.

Malachi 3:10 and 11 says,

> **Bring ye all the tithes into the storehouse, that there may be meat in mine house, and prove me now herewith, saith the Lord of hosts, if I will not open you the windows of heaven, and pour you out a blessing, that there shall not be room enough to receive it. And I will rebuke the devourer for your sakes, and he shall not destroy the fruits of your ground; neither shall your vine cast her fruit before the time in the field, saith the Lord of hosts.**

According to Malachi 3:10 and 11, when we give our tithes to the Lord, God rebukes the devil, essentially saying to him, "Hey, I'm going to deal with you *Myself*!" When we open our hands to give, God opens His mouth on our behalf!

Malachi 3:11 continues, "…he [the devourer] shall not destroy the fruits of your ground; neither shall your vine cast her fruit before the time in the field, saith the Lord of hosts."

Our giving opens the windows of Heaven, and as a result, God begins to pour financial blessings into our house. God opens His mouth and reprimands the devil, saying, "Get your hands off the finances of these givers. They are tithers, and you need to move off!" There is no rebuke like the rebuke that comes from the mouth of God Himself.

Spiritual Taste Buds for Tithing

In the previous lesson we discussed developing our children's tastebuds for the things of God. Even in the area of tithing, we need to develop the tastebuds of our children because when they are old, they will not depart from it (*see* Proverbs 22:6).

On the program, Rick shared the following story:

When I was growing up, I wasn't given tastebuds for tithing and giving. My father did not regularly tithe. In fact, my father always wanted to be a deacon in our church, but he wasn't considered because he did not tithe. My parents had many arguments over the issue of tithing. Because of his income, my father simply did not see a way to give. He had no understanding that when we give, it comes back to us. He had no revelation of sowing and reaping. We were cursed because my father didn't understand the principle of tithing. It isn't that God curses us if we don't tithe. When we remove ourselves from the cycle of blessing by not tithing, it opens a door for the devil to enter in.

Because I did not learn to tithe when I was young, after Denise and I married, I struggled with the issue of giving and tithing. I didn't want Denise to know I was not giving or tithing. She would sometimes ask, "Rick, are we tithing?" To avoid the question, I would say, "Denise, how can you possibly even ask me such a question?" I was just deflecting. I didn't want to answer her question because I knew I was being disobedient. The fact is, Denise and I lived in poverty. The devil was right in the middle of our financial situation.

Before tithing, many times, we didn't even have enough money to buy groceries. One week, I ran out of gas *five times*! I only had enough money to buy one dollar of gas at a time! I can remember praying that I would be able to drive that car on the fumes of gas. It was humiliating each time I ran out of gas to have to call someone on a pay phone to ask for them to bring me a gallon of gas. Denise and I were living in a cursed situation.

But the moment I confessed to Denise, 'I repent for not tithing. I repent for not giving. I have opened the door for this horrible poverty to dominate our lives,' I began to give, but it wasn't easy. I thought, *How can I give? We have so little.* I was tempted not to give, but then I decided that giving from the little we had wouldn't make much of a difference, and I decided it was better to obey God. As we began to tithe, little-by-little, over a period of time, we began to see our financial situation change. God began to open His mouth and rebuke the devourer for our sakes!

When we tithe, God demands that the devil get his hands off of our money. If you find that you are being devoured financially, and you are not giving tithes and offerings, you need to become a giver! When you give, God gets involved in your situation, and the door that allowed the devil into your finances is closed shut.

Develop a Budget

In addition to tithing, it is very important for us to learn how to manage our finances. We need to be mindful about what we are spending.

On the program, Rick shared this story about his own experience with budgeting and managing money:

> When I was growing up, we didn't have much money. I can remember being able to go shopping once a year to buy a new pair of jeans and a new pair of shoes. Everything else I wore were hand-me-downs that came from a woman who worked with my mother at a medical clinic. My mother would walk in the door from work with a brown paper sack filled with hand-me-downs from her coworkers family. I would be so thankful because we could not afford to shop for new clothes.
>
> We lived with a poverty mentality because of lack. I remember one time when my father I and went to the state fair. My father gave me one dollar, and I remember thinking, *What can you do with a dollar at the state fair?* Another time, my sister and I wanted to fly to New York City because my father worked for an airline and we could fly cheaply. Our budget was three dollars! Back then, that was possible, but our expectations were so limited because we didn't have much money.
>
> The only thing I knew about money was that it created stress and problems. I remember wanting to apologize to my parents if I needed new jeans or new shoes once a year because I knew it would create a financial hardship for them.
>
> When Denise and I got married, I had no clue about handling money. It wasn't that I was dumb, it was that no one had ever taught me about money. Denise and I didn't make much, but

when I got money, I spent it. We would go out to eat even though we didn't have the money to do so.

Finally, I chose to submit to authority in the area of finances. There was a man in our church who lovingly sat down with Denise and me and put us on an envelope system. The idea was to put money into designated envelopes, (food, gas, utilities, etc.), each month. Once an envelope was empty, we could not borrow from any of the other envelopes. This method caused us to really think about what we could or could not spend. It helped us create a brand new way of thinking.

It is important to understand that if you create a budget, you need to live according to that budget. You must be consistent. You can't choose to follow it one day and opt out of it the next day. If you live according to the plan, eventually you will have more money than you thought you needed.

In response to our giving, the windows of Heaven are opened and God opens His mouth to rebuke the devil, commanding him to take his hands off of our finances. When we obey God's Word, it slams the door shut, closing access to the devil into every area of our lives, including the area of finance.

God Supplies the Need of the Giver

Philippians 4:19 is a familiar verse to many Christians.

But my God shall supply all your need according to His riches in glory by Christ Jesus.

But this verse is not a promise from God to everyone. Paul was writing to the Philippians, who were his partners. They had given to Paul's ministry, and in response to their giving, Paul said, "My God shall supply all your need."

The *Rener Interpretive Version* (*RIV*) of Philippians 4:19 says,

But my God will supply all your needs so completely that He will eliminate all your deficiencies. He will meet all your physical, tangible needs until you're so full, you have no more capacity to hold anything else. He will supply all your needs until you're totally filled, packed full, and overflowing to the point of bursting at the seams and spilling over.

This promise was given to people who had just given an offering. It is equivalent to saying, "Because of what you have given, now here is what God is going to do for you." When you give tithes and offerings, you have the right to claim the promise of provision in Philippians 4:19 for yourself. That is so powerful!

If we give tithes and offerings and stick with a financial plan, we can stop the devil from finding access to our personal finances!

QUESTIONS AND ANSWERS WITH RICK RENNER

In the program, Rick answered the following question from one of our viewers.

Q. What is gossip?

A. In Second Corinthians 12:20, the apostle Paul described really bad behavior in the church at Corinth. He was fearful that when he arrived in Corinth, he might find debates, envy, wrath, strife, backbiting, whisperers, swellings, and tumults.

The word "whisperers" is the Greek word for gossip. Gossip is something you know you shouldn't be talking about, and that is the reason you whisper it rather than talk about it out loud.

Where does gossip usually happen? It happens behind closed doors or in a corner of a room where no one is listening. Gossip is whispering about business that has nothing to do with you and is not something that you can do anything about.

My rule is, if you can't say it out loud, then you ought not be saying it at all because gossiping is really just whispering about business that has nothing to do with you.

STUDY QUESTIONS

Study to shew thyself approved unto God, a workman that needeth not to be ashamed, rightly dividing the word of truth.
— 2 Timothy 2:15

1. According to John 10:10, what is the devil's plan for your life?

2. Read Malachi 3:7-11. Who will rebuke the devourer on your behalf when you become a tither?

3. Read Philippians 4:14-19. What is the promise found in this passage and who is it for?

PRACTICAL APPLICATION

**But be ye doers of the word, and not hearers only,
deceiving your own selves.
—James 1:22**

1. Think about your own upbringing. Was the principle of tithing instilled in you? How has that impacted your current financial practices?

2. Pray and ask God to identify any changes needing to be made to your financial habits. What will you do *today* to begin implementing those changes?

LESSON 8

TOPIC

Prohibit Bitterness and Unforgiveness

SCRIPTURES

1. **Proverbs 14:30** — A sound heart is the life of the flesh: but envy the rottenness of the bones.

2. **Hebrews 12:15** — Looking diligently lest any man fail of the grace of God; lest any root of bitterness springing up trouble you, and thereby many be defiled.

3. **Luke 6:45 (*NKJV*)** — For out of the abundance of the heart his mouth speaks.

4. **Luke 17:1** — It is impossible but that offences will come: but woe unto him, through whom they come!

5. **Luke 17:3** — Take heed to yourselves: If thy brother trespass against thee, rebuke him; and if he repent, forgive him.

GREEK WORDS

1. "root" — ῥίζα (*rhidza*): a root system that is very deep
2. "springing up" — φύω (*phuo*): a small plant that pierces its way through the soil
3. "trouble" — ἐνοχλέω (*enochleo*): harassed, hounded, or troubled; denotes something that bothers and upsets someone; pictures a stalker
4. "offense" — σκάνδαλον (*skandalon*): scandalous, a term used to describe the trapping of an animal; the idea of entrapment
5. "trespass" — ἁμαρτάνω (*hamartano*): to miss the mark, to make a mistake, to fall short of what is right and wrong, or to fail to meet expectations
6. "forgive" — ἀφίημι (*aphiemi*): to forgive, to disregard, or to let it go; to permanently dismiss; to release

SYNOPSIS

We have been learning about ways to block the devil from finding an entrance into our life. So far, we have discussed the following seven steps in our previous lessons:

1. Become a Child of God
2. Receive the Baptism in the Holy Spirit
3. Pray and Read Your Bible
4. Have Strengthening Relationships
5. Protect Your Marriage
6. Invest Spiritually In Your Children
7. Give Tithes and Offerings and Be Careful How You Spend

In this lesson, we will study how to prohibit bitterness and unforgiveness in our lives and close the door to the devil.

The emphasis of this lesson:

The devil is looking for access to any area in our life where we have not blocked his way. In this lesson, we will examine step number eight in our study, which is to prohibit bitterness and unforgiveness. One of the devil's most common schemes is to use unforgiveness and bitterness against us — and we *must* guard against it.

Give No Place

Proverbs 14:30 says,

A sound heart is the life of the flesh: But envy the rottenness of the bones.

By definition, the word "bitterness" is associated with envy. Doctors have noted that attitudes like unforgiveness, envy, and bitterness have an adverse effect on our health. When individuals get free of these negative attitudes, very often, their bodies become well again. The devil is looking for a way to attack us in every area of our life, and one area he especially likes to severely attack is our health.

Deep Roots

Hebrews 12:15 starts with the words, "Looking diligently...." This phrase is from the Greek word *episkopos*, which means *to look over, to manage*, or *to give oversight to*. It carries the idea that you must be very diligent about looking at your own heart. The verse continues, "...lest any man fail of the grace of God; lest any root of bitterness springing up trouble you, and thereby many be defiled."

The word "root" is the Greek word *rhidza*, which describes *a root system that is very deep*. Friend, bitterness is a very deep issue. One person with bitterness in his heart can pass that bitterness to his children; his children can pass that bitterness down to their children. If it is not dealt with, it can be an issue for *generations*. In the end, it is possible that an entire generation be bitter about a very distant generation they never even met — bitter because a root of bitterness was passed down from one generation to the next.

It is easy to take on the bitterness of another person. Have you ever found yourself feeling bitter toward someone because of what he or she did to a friend of yours? That person may not have even done anything to you personally, but you ended up feeling bitter on your friend's behalf.

It is vital to understand that the root word connected to the word "bitterness" describes something with very, very deep roots. When bitterness begins to grow in the heart, it sends its tentacles deep down into the soil of our heart.

What Is Springing up in Your Heart?

The last part of Hebrews 12:15 says, "...lest any root of bitterness springing up trouble you, and thereby many be defiled."

According to this verse, the way we know we have bitterness in our heart is that it begins to spring up. The phrase "spring up" is the Greek word *phuo*, which describes a little plant that begins to pierce its way up through the soil. When it first begins to peek up through the soil, it doesn't look very big. However, the fact that we can see it sprouting through the soil means there is a seed that is taking root and giving it life.

The way to identify if a root of bitterness is springing up in your heart is to examine how you are thinking. It is almost like we have put on a set of glasses that magnify everything in a person we don't like. Our thinking becomes colored through offense. At one time we may have enjoyed being around them, but because of offense, we are only able to see them through the lens of our bitterness. We can no longer see anything positive about them. Our distorted thinking is evidence of something in our heart — a root that needs to be removed so it doesn't spread to others.

What Is Your Mouth Speaking?

Another way to determine if you have a root of bitterness in your heart is by listening to what is coming out of your mouth. Luke 6:45 tells us, " For out of the abundance of the heart his mouth speaks."

According to Jesus, whatever is in our heart will come out of our mouth. If you want to determine what is in someone's heart, just be quiet and let them talk because their mouth will give them away. The mouth will always reveal what is in the heart.

If a person is full of himself, everything he talks about will focus on himself. If a person's heart is full of thoughts about his children, that is what will flow from him mouth. If a person is filled with love for the Lord, he will talk about the Lord.

Our mouth is an outlet for our heart, and if we have a root of bitterness, there is no way to keep bitterness from coming out — at some point, that bitterness *will* spew from our mouth. Suddenly we will begin to say things that are not worthy of our mouth. Without restraint, we will begin speaking terrible things about others because there is a root of bitterness down deep that is beginning to trouble us.

What Is Troubling You?

Again, Hebrews 12:15 says, "…lest any root of bitterness springing up trouble you, and thereby many be defiled." The Greek word for "trouble" is *enochleo* and it means *to harass, to hound,* or *to trouble.* It denotes *something that bothers and upsets someone to the extreme.* The English word "stalker" also describes this word.

When a root of bitterness begins to spring up, the person with bitterness is filled with offense and hounded by thoughts of the person who offended him. Thoughts about something another person did or did not do stalk the one with bitterness. Unforgiveness and bitterness will open a door for the devil to wiggle his way into the life of the one offended and will affect their mind, their emotions, and their health. Eventually the devil will completely ravage their life.

Offense Will Come

It is so important to understand how detrimental bitterness and offense are to our welfare. Jesus said in Luke 17:1, "It is impossible but that offenses will come: but woe unto him, through whom they come!"

Jesus was saying, "You may as well learn how to deal with this because in this life and in this world where you constantly rub elbows with other people, there will always be the potential of being offended."

The word translated "offenses" is the Greek word *skandalon* from which the English word "scandal" is derived. It was a term used to describe *the trapping of an animal* and carries the idea of *entrapment.* A *skandalon* was a little piece of wood that held the upper part of a trap in place. Hunters would bait the trap by putting a piece of food inside the trap. When an animal came along and walked into the trap, it would accidentally bump the *skandalon* and cause the trap to collapse, entrapping the animal.

Two Reasons for Offense

When we discuss offense, the idea behind it is *entrapment.* The devil is doing all he can do to entrap people with offense. There are two main reasons people become offended. First, many people become offended because of what someone did or said to them. Second, many people become offended because of what someone did *not* do or say to them.

Offense can be the result of someone disappointing us and doing something below our expectations. Have you ever gone through something difficult in life and expected someone to reach out to you with a phone call, visit, text message, or email, but no one did? Many of us would feel disappointed because we expected more of the people in our lives.

The truth is, we have probably similarly disappointed someone in our lifetime. Someone probably expected something of us, and we failed to meet that expectation. If that is the case, did you intend to offend that individual? Probably not. You may have learned that you caused someone to be offended and may have been shocked by it and wondered how that person could think that of you because you would never intentionally hurt or disappoint someone. We want those people to believe the best in us, not the worst.

In the same way, we need to believe the best of the people who have failed to meet our expectations. It is doubtful that an individual woke up one morning and said, "Today, I'm going to do my best to offend this person." That is very unlikely. But if we are ignorant of the wiles of the wicked one, the devil may whisper, "Oh, wow! Listen to what that person said about you. Look how he treated you. What a disappointment! Don't you expect him to be better than that? He did nothing for you in your time of need. What a lousy person he is! What a great disappointment!" Listening to and being convinced by the devil's lies is how we become entrapped in offense. It becomes a *skandalon* in our soul.

Take Heed to Yourselves

The word "offense" also means *to trip or stumble* or *to lose one's footing*. When we have been offended, it can cause us to trip, stumble, or lose our footing spiritually. When someone has offended us repeatedly, most of us want us to lash out at them. But Jesus instructed His followers to respond differently. In Luke 17:3, Jesus said,

> **Take heed to yourselves: If thy brother trespass against thee, rebuke him; and if he repent, forgive him.**

The Greek meaning of the phrase "take heed," means *to get a grip on yourself*. Jesus addressed our tendency to want to *get a grip* on someone who has offended us, but He instructs us to get a grip on *ourselves*. When we are ready to pounce on someone in retaliation for an offense, Jesus is saying, "Wait, wait, wait. Put everything on pause. Get a grip on yourself. Give yourself time to calm down. Take a pause and become more peaceful."

Luke 17:3 continues, "…If thy brother trespass against thee, rebuke him…." The word "trespass" is the Greek word *hamartano*, meaning *to make a mistake, fail to meet your expectations* or *to fall short of what was right and wrong in any given situation*. When we are wronged, Jesus instructs us to "rebuke" the one who has fallen short. The word "rebuke" is the Greek word *epitimao*, which has the idea of *confrontation*.

Confrontation can either be cruel or it can be kind. If we approach confrontation with the motive of retaliation, it will have a negative effect. But if we approach confrontation with reconciliation in our heart, it will lead to healing. We need to examine our motives when we have to rebuke a brother or sister to be sure we are approaching the conflict with an attitude of reconciliation.

Let It Go

In the last portion of Luke 17:3 Jesus said, "…If he repents, forgive him." The word "forgive" is the Greek word, *aphiemi*. This word literally means *let it go; permanently dismiss; to send so far away that you can never reach over to retrieve it and bring it up again; to forfeit the right to ever mention it again.* When someone does something that has the potential to bring offense in our lives, we need to let it go. If someone who has offended us asks for forgiveness, we are required by Jesus to let it go and permanently dismiss it, and we forfeit the right to ever mention the offense again.

The very same word is used to describe how God has forgiven us. When Jesus forgives us, He forfeits his right to ever bring our past sins up to us again. He literally dismisses our past, sends it away, and lets it go.

If we refuse to let go of offense, the door will be opened for the devil to wiggle his way into our thoughts, our emotions, and our health to ultimately take us down.

When we step into that position where we let go of an offense we have received from someone, healing and reconciliation can begin to flow back into that relationship and we completely shut the door to the devil.

We began this lesson with Proverbs 14:30 which says,

A sound heart is the life of the flesh: but envy the rottenness of the bones.

Many people, even believers, have sickness in their body as a result of envy, unforgiveness, and bitterness. We can close the door to the devil by simply getting a grip on ourself, confronting people with a heart of reconciliation, and if they ask forgiveness, obeying Jesus' command to just let it go.

QUESTIONS AND ANSWERS WITH RICK RENNER

In the program, Rick answered the following question from one of our viewers.

Q. Why do Christians go through spiritual deserts?

A. I've been through a few spiritual deserts myself, and it just seems that those are times when your spiritual life feels dry. But in those moments in my life, I've hit my knees and opened my Bible. I begin to seek the face of God to pour heavenly showers out on my life.

Rather than say, "Oh, it's just so spiritually dry and I don't feel anything right now," turn that into a moment when you begin to seek the face of God. And my friends, God will respond to you.

Jeremiah 33:3 promises that if you call out to God in faith, He will hear you. He will answer you and He will show you great and mighty things.

If you feel like you're in a spiritually dry place, hit your knees, begin to seek the face of God, open your Bible, dive in deep, and ask God to pour a heavenly shower out on your life, and you will begin to blossom again.

STUDY QUESTIONS

Study to shew thyself approved unto God, a workman that needeth not to be ashamed, rightly dividing the word of truth.
— 2 Timothy 2:15

1. Study and meditate on Proverbs 14:30. Explain what it means to have a "sound heart."
2. Describe the Greek meaning of the word "root" found in Hebrews 12:15.
3. Read Acts 7:51-60 and note the similarities between Stephen's act of forgiveness and Jesus' declaration on the cross in Luke 23:26-34

PRACTICAL APPLICATION

> But be ye doers of the word, and not hearers only,
> deceiving your own selves.
> —James 1:22

1. Review the meaning of the word "forgive" found in Luke 17:3. Examine your heart and ask the Holy Spirit to reveal any unknown bitterness that may have taken root in your heart.

2. Read Hebrews 12:14 and 15. Seeking peace doesn't always mean the restoration of a relationship, since more than one person's free will is involved. But it does mean the removal of bitterness, offense, and strife by choosing to forgive. What steps do you need to take to remove bitterness from your heart and avoid the trap of offense in the future?

LESSON 9

TOPIC

Eat Right and Exercise

SCRIPTURES

1. **1 Corinthians 9:26** — I therefore so run, not as uncertainly; so fight I, not as one that beateth the air

2. **1 Thessalonians 4:4** — That every one of you should know how to possess his vessel in sanctification and honour

GREEK WORDS

1. "run" — τρέχω (*trecho*): to run; pictures one who has jumped into the race and is pressing ahead with all his might to reach a goal set before him; one who is running at such a pace that both feet never hit the ground at the same time; with eyes fixed on the finish line, the runner makes a run for it, steadily moving forward toward the goal

2. "uncertainly" — ἄδηλος (*adelos*): uncertainly; aimlessly; without direction; having no aim, no plan

3. "fight" — πυκτεύω (*pukteuo*): pictures a boxer; used only here in the New Testament, and depicts a boxer who gives a knock-out punch

4. "possess" — κτάομαι (*ktaomai*): control; manage; possess; to win the mastery over

SYNOPSIS

Most of us would never think of a poor diet and a lack of exercise as an avenue for the devil to gain access into our lives, but it is. The next step to block the devil from our lives is eating right and exercising. Obesity is a huge problem in today's world, and many are wracked with sickness and disease, directly resulting from unhealthy eating and lack of exercise. In First Corinthians 9, Paul said that he did not run his race with uncertainty, but with discipline. In First Thessalonians 4:4 he said that we are to know how to control our own body. It is time for us to make the decision to eat a healthy diet and to exercise so our life will not be cut short and we can accomplish God's purpose for our lives.

The emphasis of this lesson:

It takes planning to begin eating a healthy diet and exercising regularly. We must be determined to close every door and window that would allow the devil access into our physical bodies and possibly shorten God's plan for our lives. In this lesson, we will learn how to close the door to the devil and keep him out of our body and our health.

The number of people today who are living on medication, including those who belong to the Body of Christ and believe that by His stripes we are healed, is shocking. People today are highly medicated and are dealing with all types of health issues. Jesus died to provide healing and health. So why are so many people sick today? Obviously, a huge door is open, and the devil is entering through that door to wreak havoc on the health of God's people.

Rick Renner's Personal Journey

On the program, Rick shares his testimony:

> In a previous lesson, I shared that when I was a young boy, my mother did not feed us healthy food. I thought really good food was greasy, fried, junky food. Give me a baloney sandwich with

lots of Miracle Whip. Give me potato chips or anything greasy and fried. I loved eating a diet of these foods. Over the years, that is the way I had regularly eaten. Through the years, I gained weight, lost weight, and gained weight over and over again. I have been on all kinds of crazy diets. On one diet, I ate nothing but watermelon. During that diet I was with Joyce Meyer, and she asked, "Rick, how are you losing weight?" to which I responded, "I don't eat anything but watermelon." Joyce lovingly responded, "Rick, you cannot live only on watermelon."

Over the years, I probably lost thousands of pounds on extreme diets, but I could never keep it off. I learned how to drape my body in black clothes to try to hide the bulges and rolls, but I just kept getting bigger and bigger. I finally had gained so much weight I weighed 340 pounds! The devil was literally ravaging me. I was failing.

There was one time when I had flown to Riga, Latvia to visit the pastor of one of our churches. While in a hotel, I fell. I was so heavy at that time that I couldn't get off of the floor without help. I was crumbling in my health.

The truth is that the devil was ravaging me because of the way I was eating. I could have shut the door to the devil. It was all preventable, but I allowed it because I wasn't properly managing myself.

Finally, one Thanksgiving, we were all gathered around the table eating and I just dove into the turkey and all of the other food. I was eating like there was no end to the food in sight. My family just watched and let me dive in, but when dinner was over, my son said, 'Hey Dad, we need to talk to you about something.'

We went into another room, they closed the door, and I knew this was going to be serious. My sons said, "You are going to have a change in your life starting tomorrow. You're going on a diet, and you are going to begin an exercise program." I was so angry that I threatened to fire two of my sons. I told Denise she had no right to tell me what I was going to do with my life or my body. I was fuming. But my family loved me enough to confront me.

The next day, my life changed. I began eating differently. I began to exercise. Until that time, the word "exercise" was like a four-letter word. I didn't want to go anywhere *near* the subject of exercise. I had never exercised as a young man. I had never exercised as an adult.

Over the years, I had flirted with the idea of exercise. Denise and I even bought exercise equipment. We bought a treadmill that we never used. It sat in the TV room and became a great place to hang our excess clothes. Then we bought a trampoline, and it became a makeshift bookshelf for the books that I didn't have room for on my actual bookshelves. We couldn't use the trampoline because it was stacked with books. We couldn't use the treadmill because it was covered with clothes. We were considering the idea of exercise, but we never made the decision to change.

That moment finally came when I realized that if I was going to be healthy to the end of my life — if I was going to be around for Denise and my sons and my grandkids and you, my friends God has called me to minister to — then I had to make a change or I was going to cut my life short.

I have no judgment for anyone who has struggled with the issue of weight. I've been there, I've done that, and Jesus gave me the victory! It took that confrontation by my family to cause me to seek the face of God and ultimately make a decision to change my lifestyle and shut the door to the enemy.

It is interesting that some doctors now say that 90 percent of sicknesses are diet related. That means, if we eat right, we may be able to remedy 90 percent of sicknesses. It is possible that by eating right, we may be able to bring correction to most of what is ailing our body.

Many people go about their lives and do nothing to move their bodies. As a result, they become immobile very early in life. That is not the will of God for you or for anybody else, but you can stop it. You can block the enemy from ravaging your health by simply taking some positive steps to do what is right.

Eyes Fixed on the Finish Line

In First Corinthians 9:26, Paul said,

I therefore so run, not as uncertainly; so fight I, not as one that beateth the air.

The Greek word for "run" is *treho*, which literally means *to run*. The word pictures one who has jumped into the race and is pressing ahead with all of his might to reach a goal that is set before him. It describes one who is running at such a pace that both feet never hit the ground at the same time; with eyes fixed on the finish line, the runner makes a run for it, steadily moving forward toward the goal.

On the program, Rick explained that when he began to change his diet and exercise, this verse became very important to him because he understood he didn't have to reach the goal immediately. He realized he needed to begin making steady movement toward developing a lifestyle of moving his body, regaining mobility, and exercising.

Begin With Small Goals

If you are determined to close the door to the devil in regard to your weight, begin with a small goal. Do not begin with something that is not attainable. Begin with something achievable. Once you reach your first goal, move your goal a little bit further and make it a little higher. As you achieve each goal, keep moving your goal further out, step by step. If you continue day by day, you will reach a point where you look back and say to yourself, "Wow, I have lost a lot of weight," But you didn't do it in a week, you didn't do it in a month. You did it one step at a time as you steadily kept pushing the goal further and further out.

To be successful, you must keep your eyes fixed on those goals. You must be serious about what you will do in regard to exercise. Your goal shouldn't be to become an Olympic athlete. For a large majority of people, that goal would be unrealistic and unachievable. Simply make an achievable goal like taking a five-minute walk or walking up a flight of stairs. If you haven't exercised in a long time, this would be a good way to begin. If you cannot make it up an entire flight of stairs, just do as many as you are physically able to do. Do that each day until you are ready to move the goal. If you start out with a goal of regularly taking five-minute walks and achieve that, increase it to ten minutes, then to fifteen minutes, and then to thirty minutes. You may even work up to walking for an hour. Determine to steadily move forward and regain your health.

Change Requires a Plan

When Paul said, "I therefore so run not as uncertainly," it indicates that he had a plan. The word "uncertainly" is the Greek word *adelos*, which means *uncertainly, aimlessly, without direction, having no aim, no goal, and no plan.* It is important to understand that if we don't have a plan, we will not make progress. If we just try to figure things out along the way, we will not succeed. We will continue eating the way we have always eaten and avoid exercise as we always have.

Watching what we eat and exercising will take discipline. In order to truly succeed, we need the Holy Spirit working in our life. Discipline is a fruit of the Spirit. We need a plan. Our plan must be attainable for both weight loss and exercise, which will require discipline. Begin at an attainable level and work your way toward a greater goal with incremental goals along the way.

The Knockout Punch

Paul continues, "…I therefore so run, not as uncertainly; so fight I, not as one that beateth the air." The Greek word for "fight" is *pukteuo* and depicts a boxer. This word occurs only in this passage. The word depicts *a boxer who gives a knockout punch.* If you are struggling in this area of your life, you must understand that *God wants you to overcome!* He wants you to decimate the enemy that is trying to destroy you.

Gain Mastery Over Your Vessel

My friends, it requires a decision on your part if you want to slam the door shut on the devil and block him from gaining access into your body and your health.

In First Thessalonians 4:4, Paul says, "That every one of you should know how to possess his vessel in sanctification and honor." The word "possess" is the Greek word *ktaomai* and means *to control, to manage, to possess* or *to win mastery over.*

If your body has been calling the shots, and your flesh has convinced you to eat everything and anything you want to eat — if you have been undisciplined concerning your body — you will need to be determined to win mastery over it. You will need to learn how to control, manage, and gain mastery over your body. It may require you to read books or listen to an audio series that can help you gain understanding. What is important is learning spiritually and naturally how to gain mastery over your physical body.

Once when Rick was being interviewed, he was asked, "What is the worst enemy you have ever had to overcome?" He paused and answered, "Me." If we can overcome ourselves, we can do anything. This is true for everyone. We need to gain mastery over our vessel.

The word "vessel" in First Thessalonians 4:4 describes the human body. It is also the word to describe *an instrument*. If an instrument hasn't been used for a long time, it can become unusable. It can become rusty or corroded. The instrument may have had the potential to be a great instrument, but because it was left alone, it becomes nearly unusable. For that instrument to be useable again, it will require some work. The same is true of our physical body.

When we allow the devil access into our body by overeating and never exercising, we can only imagine him saying, "Hip-hip hooray! As long as they keep eating that junk food and never get off the couch, I can wreak havoc in their physical body and knock them out of their race early in life!"

Perhaps you have been claiming and confessing long life over yourself. That is great, but it is also important that you change the way you eat and start moving your body. If you continue doing what you have been doing, you will never achieve your goal.

You can close the door right now. It is time for you to say, "I am done with leaving the door opened for the devil to wreak havoc on my body. I am making the decision today to change the way I eat. I am making the decision today to begin exercising, and by setting incremental goals, I will keep pushing forward to lose excess weight and gain more mobility until I achieve it."

These are such vital decisions I encourage you to make. You won't regret your decision.

QUESTIONS AND ANSWERS WITH RICK RENNER

In the program, Rick answered the following question from one of our viewers.

Rick, did you read your Bible today?

The answer is yes. In fact, it is so important to me that I begin my day reading the Bible. I have even empowered my team around me to daily ask me, "Did you read your Bible today?" I never begin my day without first making it a priority to take the Word of God into my life to feed my inner man every single day.

It is amazing that people eat food because they know if they don't eat, they will become weak. In the very same way, if we don't feed our spirit, we will become spiritually weak. My friends, it is simply not wise to start your day without taking the Word of God into your life every day. I encourage you to make that decision today.

STUDY QUESTIONS

Study to shew thyself approved unto God, a workman that needeth not to be ashamed, rightly dividing the word of truth.
— 2 Timothy 2:15

1. Define the meaning of "uncertainly" found in First Corinthians 9:26. If there is an area in your life in which you have been running uncertainly, how will you change the way you have been running your race?
2. Describe in detail the meaning of the Greek word *pukteuo* for "I fight" found in First Corinthians 9:26.
3. In First Thessalonians 4:4, Paul instructed us to possess or to win mastery over our "vessel" (body). Explain why this is important for living successfully as a follower of Jesus Christ.

PRACTICAL APPLICATION

But be ye doers of the word, and not hearers only, deceiving your own selves.
— James 1:22

1. Take a moment to identify an area in your life where you need to possess, control, manage, or win mastery over your body (*see* 1 Thessalonians 4:4). Describe how you will accomplish this.

TOPIC

Be Filled With the Spirit and Resist the Devil

SCRIPTURES

1. **Ephesians 6:10,11** — Finally, my brethren, be strong in the Lord, and in the power of his might. Put on the whole armour of God, that ye may be able to stand against the wiles of the devil.

2. **James 4:7** — Submit yourselves therefore to God. Resist the devil, and he will flee from you.

3. **James 4:7 (*RIV*)** — It is imperative you make the decision to properly align yourselves under the authority of God — a submitted position that provides you with protection. And being submitted to His authority gives you the ability to defy, to oppose, to stand steadfastly against, and to withstand the accusing, slanderous, trap-setting behavior of the devil. In fact, he'll be so terrified of your resistance that he'll move his feet as fast as he can to get away from you. Not only will he flee from you, he'll run like a criminal terrified of prosecution — so scared that he'll want to do all he can to put as much space between him and you as possible.

GREEK WORDS

1. "be strong" — ἐνδύω (*enduo*): compound of ἐν (*en*) and δύναμις (*dunamis*); the word ἐν (*en*) means in, and δύναμις (*dunamis*) means power and depicts the forces of an entire army; but when these words are compounded, it pictures the power of a whole army being deposited into a person; an inner strengthening; a supernatural enablement; pictures explosive, superhuman power that comes with enormous

energy and produces phenomenal, extraordinary, and unparalleled results being deposited into a receptacle

2. "may be able" — δύναμαι (*dunamai*): to empower, to have divine ability

3. "to stand" — στῆναι (*stenai*): to stand upright

4. "against" — πρός (*pros*): against; denotes a forward position or a face-to-face encounter

5. "wiles" — μεθοδεία (*methodeia*): a compound of μετά (*meta*), meaning with, and ὁδός (*hodos*), meaning avenue, path, or road; as a compound, means with a road, to operate on an avenue, or to travel on a specific route; this portrays direction and objective; direction or strategy; conveys craftiness and deceit; where we get the word method

6. "submit" — ὑποτάσσω (*hupotasso*): a compound of ὑπό (*hupo*) and τάσσω (*tasso*); the preposition ὑπό (*hupo*) means under, and the word τάσσω (*tasso*) means to arrange; to properly align yourselves under authority; a submitted position that provides you with protection; a military term depicting a solider's obedience and submission to authority; pictures one who is submitted to authority as being under the covering and protection of a greater authority, and that actually hides him behind the authority of the one to whom he is submitted; this tells us that there is protection in submission; in context, signifies one who properly arranges himself under the authority of God and His Word

7. "resist" — ἀνθίστημι (*anthistemi*): a compound of ἀντί (*anti*) and ἵστημι (*histemi*); the word ἀντί (*anti*) means against, and the word ἵστημι (*histemi*) means to stand; demonstrates the attitude of one who is fiercely opposed to something and therefore determines to do everything within his power to resist it; to defy, to stand against, or to withstand; it depicts a well-thought-out and well-planned resistance; used to picture the fierce resistance of an enemy; to stand steadfastly against or to withstand

8. "devil" — διάβολος (*diabolos*): accusing, slanderous, trap-setting devil; portrays one who is known to slander, accuse, assault, or who tries to ensnare others in some kind of a net or trap

9. "flee" — φεύγω (*pheugo*): to flee, to take flight, to run away, to run as fast as possible, or to escape; pictures one's feet flying as he runs from a situation; used to depict a lawbreaker who flees in terror from a city or a nation where he broke the law; on rarer occasions, it could mean

to be charged with a crime, or to be exiled; it means to be so terrified that one will move his feet to run as fast as he can, running like a scared criminal terrified of prosecution

SYNOPSIS

The devil is searching for any entry point he can find into our lives. He is a thief and wants to steal whatever he can in the areas of our health, our finances, our marriage, our children, and our jobs. If we do not fortify our lives with God's Word and prayer, the devil will find a way in. The steps we have already reviewed include:

1. Become a Child of God
2. Receive the Baptism in the Holy Spirit
3. Pray and Read Your Bible
4. Have Strengthening Relationships
5. Protect Your Marriage
6. Invest Spiritually in Your Children
7. Give Tithes and Offerings and Be Careful How You Spend Money
8. Give No Place to Bitterness and Unforgiveness
9. Eat Right and Exercise

In our final lesson, we will discuss how we can be filled with the Spirit and strengthened to resist the devil.

The emphasis of this lesson:

By the Holy Spirit, God has divinely enabled His children to stand against every scheme of the devil. As we resist the devil and are in submission to God's authority, he will and must flee from us!

Don't Give Place to the Devil

In John 10:10, Jesus says the devil is a thief and he comes to steal, kill, and destroy. He can't help himself. His nature is twisted and bent. If we don't block him, he will find an entrance into our life. But we have the power to push him out of every area of our life where he is trying to gain entrance.

In Ephesians 6:10, the apostle Paul said, "Finally my brethren...." The word "finally" in the original Greek means *to the last and most important matter at hand.* Paul was about to share something very important: "...Be strong in the Lord and in the power of his might."

The word "strong" is translated from the Greek word *enduo.* It is a compound of two words. The first word is *en* which means *in,* as in *putting a substance inside a vessel.* The second word is *duo,* which is the word for *power.* It is also a derivative of the word *dunamis,* which describes *the full might of an advancing army.* When these two words are put together they form the word *enduo,* which describes *a power that is placed inside of some kind of receptacle.* It depicts *the forces of an entire army.* This is *an inner strengthening* or *a supernatural enablement.* When God puts His mighty power on the inside of us, we suddenly become like a one-man army. We are a receptacle designed to receive an infilling of the Holy Spirit.

Be Strong in the Lord

According to this verse, when we are indued — when God fills us with the Holy Spirit — suddenly we become strong in the Lord and the power of His might. In this way we have everything at our disposal to tell the devil to hit the road! When we receive an infusion of the Holy Spirit's power, we become divinely enabled to stand against the wiles of the devil.

On the program, Rick shared this story from his own life:

> Once, many, many years ago, we were going through a rough season financially in the ministry. It seemed like our partners had stopped giving for a season, and we never knew why. I believe it was a spiritual attack. That attack became so severe that one day, I found myself in the middle of the night standing on Red Square in Moscow, Russia, crying. I was just walking around crying and saying, "Lord, You've got to do something for us. Lord, please touch me, give me insight, give me the power to deal with this." In that very moment, *enduo* — it was like God took His *dunamis* power and placed it inside me. When that power came on the inside of me, it was like Superman suddenly emerged!

That is exactly what happens when we are endued or filled with the Spirit. It changes us and divinely enables us, stand against the wiles of the devil instead of running away in fear.

A Face-to-Face Confrontation

Ephesians 6:11 says,

> **Put on the whole armour of God, that ye may be able to stand against the wiles of the devil.**

The word "stand" is the Greek word *stenai*. It describes *a soldier standing tall, his head held high, his shoulders thrown back, standing very upright, very proud with no reason to be ashamed.* The power of God puts us in a winning position to stand against the wiles of the devil.

The word "against" in Greek is the word *pros*, which describes a face-to-face confrontation. Instead of running *from*, we are now charging *toward* the fight. If the devil has found a door into our life, we need this kind of fresh infilling to charge the enemy and push him back.

The devil does not belong in our life. The first step we examined is to become a child of God. At that moment, we were translated out of the kingdom of darkness into the kingdom of God's dear Son (*see* Colossians 1:13,14) We passed from death into life (*see* 1 John 3:14). Darkness and death have no right to be in our life. When we are filled with the power of God, suddenly we are enabled to stand against the enemy face to face and push him back across the line and out of our life.

Again, Ephesians 6:11 says, "Put on the whole armour of God, that ye may be able to stand against the wiles of the devil." The word "wiles" is the Greek word *methodeias*. It is a compound of two words, the word *meta*, which means *with*, and the word *hodos*, which means *avenue, path,* or *road*. As a compound, *methodeias* means *with a road, to operate on an avenue*. It carries the idea of *strategy*. It conveys *craftiness* and *deceit*. The word "method" is derived from this Greek word, which means the devil is looking for an *inroad* into our life. He is craftily seeking an avenue to bust his way into our existence, to wiggle his way into the middle of our affairs to bring chaos.

Submit and Resist

James 4:7 says,

> **Submit yourselves therefore to God. Resist the devil, and he will flee from you.**

If you are under attack, before you begin to deal with the devil, first make sure you are submitted to the Lord. That is what this verse is saying. We must check our heart to ensure we are truly in submission to God's authority. When we are in submission to God's authority, it empowers us.

The word "submit" is the Greek word *hupotasso*. It is a compound word of *hupo* and the word *tasso*. The word *hupo* means *under*. The word *tasso* means *to arrange*. Together this word means *to properly align yourself under someone's authority; a submitted position that provides us with protection.*

Hupotasso was a military term depicting a soldier's obedience and submission to authority. It pictures one who submitted to authority as being under their covering and of being under the protection of a greater authority. This submission actually hides the individual behind the authority of the one to whom they have submitted.

In other words, there is protection in submission. In the context of James 4:7, it signifies one who properly arranges himself under the authority of God and His Word. When we are properly aligned under God, His authority and His Word empower us to hide behind Him. God becomes our protection. When we examine our heart to be sure we are properly submitted to God, we are then in a position to resist the devil, and he will flee.

The Fierce Resistance Against the Enemy

What does "resist the devil" mean? The word "resist" is a Greek word meaning *to be fiercely opposed to something, to be determined to do everything in our power to resist a thing.* The word "resist" means *defy, fiercely oppose, steadfastly stand against,* or *withstand.* And the one we are to resist is the devil!

The word "devil" is the Greek word *diabolos,* which describes *one that is accusing, slanderous, and trap-setting.* It portrays *one who is known to slander, accuse, assault or ensnare others in some type of net or a trap.* The devil will always try to accuse, slander, set traps against, and work his way into the life of a believer. So we must close *every* access point into our lives to keep him out. The Bible promises that if we resist the devil, he will flee.

The word "flee" means, *to flee, to take flight, to run away, to run as fast as possible,* or *to escape.* It pictures *one's feet flying as he runs from a situation* and was used to depict *a law breaker who flees in terror from a city or a nation where he broke the law.* On rarer occasions, it could mean *to be charged with a crime* or *to be exiled.* It means *to be so terrified that one moves his feet to run as fast as he can, running like a frightened criminal, terrified of prosecution.*

When we align ourselves under God, we are empowered to resist the devil. The devil becomes so terrified of our resistance that he flees, running away as fast as he can.

The *Renner Interpretive Version (RIV)* of James 4:7 says,

> **It is imperative you make the decision to properly align yourselves under the authority of God — a submitted position that provides you with protection. And being submitted to His authority gives you the ability to defy, to oppose, to stand steadfastly against, and to withstand the accusing, slanderous, trap-setting behavior of the devil. In fact, he'll be so terrified of your resistance that he'll move his feet as fast as he can to get away from you. Not only will he flee from you, he'll run like a criminal terrified of prosecution — so scared that he'll want to do all he can to put as much space between him and you as possible.**

Submit to the Authority of God

The devil doesn't know how to deal with a believer who is submitted to the authority of God. If the devil has already found access to our life, it probably means there is some area where we have not really been in submission to the authority of God.

In the area of our health, if we have been eating unhealthy food and have been undisciplined in exercise, the door is opened to the devil into the area of our health. Or perhaps, our finances are a mess, our marriage is struggling, or we are having problems with our children. The list can go on and on. Having problems in any of these areas is indicative of a crack somewhere in our life where we have not really submitted to the Lordship of Jesus — where the devil is being allowed to enter our lives and wreak havoc.

However, when we submit to the lordship of Jesus and say, "Lord, I'm going to submit to You," suddenly we come under His authority and protection and are empowered to resist the devil. We are divinely filled with the Spirit to stand against the wiles of the devil. If he attempts to enter any area of our life, the devil is in violation and has no right to do so.

When we submit to the Lord and resist the devil, he must flee. And when he does, he will run away terrified; he will run as fast as he can from our lives!

QUESTIONS AND ANSWERS WITH RICK RENNER

In the program, Rick answered the following question from one of our viewers.

Q. Were there actually monsters in the Old Testament?

A. We know from the book of Genesis chapter 6 that there were Nephilim in the earth. Nephilim were hybrid creatures that were born as a result of a union between fallen angels and mortal women. The women became impregnated, and they gave birth to giants, which were hybrid, fallen creatures.

Nephilim were an aberration from what God designed. There are very ancient sources that tell us the giants then had sexual intercourse with animals, and the animals gave birth to hybrid creatures that were not normal.

These were monsters that roamed the earth. It indeed is very possible that there really were monsters that roamed the earth in the days before the Flood. I write about all of this in my book, *Fallen Angels, Giants, Monsters, and the World Before the Flood.*

STUDY QUESTIONS

> Study to shew thyself approved unto God, a workman that needeth not to be ashamed, rightly dividing the word of truth.
> — 2 Timothy 2:15

1. According to Ephesians 6:11, what is the purpose of the armor of God?
2. Describe the meaning behind the words "stand against" found in Ephesians 6:11.
3. What is the meaning of the word "submit" in James 4:7, and what is the result when we obey this command?

PRACTICAL APPLICATION

But be ye doers of the word, and not hearers only,
deceiving your own selves.
—James 1:22

1. In Ephesians 6:10, Paul exhorts us to "be strong in the Lord." The word "strong" refers to an inner strengthening and supernatural enablement. Describe a time in your life when you experienced this strengthening or enablement. What was the result?

2. Examine your relationship with the Lord. In what areas do you need to submit to His lordship more fully? What changes will you make today to do so?

A Prayer To Receive Salvation

If you've never received Jesus as your Savior and Lord, now is the time for you to experience the new life Jesus wants to give you! To receive God's gift of salvation that can be obtained through Jesus alone, pray this prayer from your heart:

Jesus, I repent of my sin and receive You as my Savior and Lord. Wash away my sin with Your precious blood and make me completely new. I thank You that my sin is removed, and Satan no longer has any right to lay claim on me. Through Your empowering grace, I faithfully promise that I will serve You as my Lord for the rest of my life.

If you just prayed this prayer of salvation, you are born again! You are a brand-new creation in Christ! Would you please let us know of your decision by going to **renner.org/salvation**? We would love to connect with you and pray for you as you begin your new life in Christ.

Scriptures for further study: John 3:16; John 14:6; Acts 4:12; Ephesians 1:7; Hebrews 10:19,20; 1 Peter 1:18,19; Romans 10:9,10; Colossians 1:13; 2 Corinthians 5:17; Romans 6:4; 1 Peter 1:3

Notes

CLAIM YOUR FREE RESOURCE!

As a way of introducing you further to the teaching ministry of Rick Renner, we would like to send you FREE of charge his teaching, "How To Receive a Miraculous Touch From God" on CD or as an MP3 download.

In His earthly ministry, Jesus commonly healed *all* who were sick of *all* their diseases. In this profound message, learn about the manifold dimensions of Christ's wisdom, goodness, power, and love toward all humanity who came to Him in faith with their needs.

☑ **YES, I want to receive Rick Renner's monthly teaching letter!**

Simply scan the QR code to claim this resource or go to:
renner.org/claim-your-free-offer

Connect

WITH US!

R renner.org